Ups and Downs

Algebra

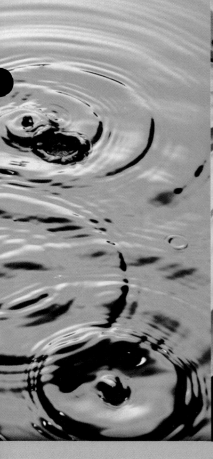

BRITANNICA
Mathematics in Context

TEACHER'S GUIDE

HOLT, RINEHART AND WINSTON

Mathematics in Context is a comprehensive curriculum for the middle grades. It was developed in 1991 through 1997 in collaboration with the Wisconsin Center for Education Research, School of Education, University of Wisconsin-Madison and the Freudenthal Institute at the University of Utrecht, The Netherlands, with the support of the National Science Foundation Grant No. 9054928.

The revision of the curriculum was carried out in 2003 through 2005, with the support of the National Science Foundation Grant No. ESI 0137414.

National Science Foundation
Opinions expressed are those of the authors
and not necessarily those of the Foundation.

Abels, M.; de Jong, J. A.; Dekker, T.; Meyer, M. R.; Shew, J. A.; Burrill, G.; and Simon, A. N. (2006). *Ups and downs*. In Wisconsin Center for Education Research & Freudenthal Institute (Eds.), Mathematics in Context. Chicago: Encyclopædia Britannica, Inc.

The Teacher's Guide for this unit was prepared by David C. Webb, Bryna Rappaport, Truus Dekker, and Dédé de Haan.

ISBN 0-03-039839-8

4 5 6   073   09 08 07

The *Mathematics in Context* Development Team

Development 1991–1997

The initial version of *Ups and Downs* was developed by Mieke Abels and Jan Auke de Jong.
It was adapted for use in American schools by Margaret R. Meyer, Julia A. Shew, Gail Burrill,
and Aaron N. Simon.

Wisconsin Center for Education

Research Staff

Thomas A. Romberg
Director

Joan Daniels Pedro
Assistant to the Director

Gail Burrill
Coordinator

Margaret R. Meyer
Coordinator

Project Staff

Jonathan Brendefur
Laura Brinker
James Browne
Jack Burrill
Rose Byrd
Peter Christiansen
Barbara Clarke
Doug Clarke
Beth R. Cole
Fae Dremock
Mary Ann Fix

Sherian Foster
James A, Middleton
Jasmina Milinkovic
Margaret A. Pligge
Mary C. Shafer
Julia A. Shew
Aaron N. Simon
Marvin Smith
Stephanie Z. Smith
Mary S. Spence

Freudenthal Institute Staff

Jan de Lange
Director

Els Feijs
Coordinator

Martin van Reeuwijk
Coordinator

Mieke Abels
Nina Boswinkel
Frans van Galen
Koeno Gravemeijer
Marja van den Heuvel-Panhuizen
Jan Auke de Jong
Vincent Jonker
Ronald Keijzer
Martin Kindt

Jansie Niehaus
Nanda Querelle
Anton Roodhardt
Leen Streefland
Adri Treffers
Monica Wijers
Astrid de Wild

Revision 2003–2005

The revised version of *Ups and Downs* was developed by Truus Dekker and Mieke Abels.
It was adapted for use in American schools by Gail Burrill.

Wisconsin Center for Education

Research Staff

Thomas A. Romberg
Director

David C. Webb
Coordinator

Gail Burrill
Editorial Coordinator

Margaret A. Pligge
Editorial Coordinator

Project Staff

Sarah Ailts
Beth R. Cole
Erin Hazlett
Teri Hedges
Karen Hoiberg
Carrie Johnson
Jean Krusi
Elaine McGrath

Margaret R. Meyer
Anne Park
Bryna Rappaport
Kathleen A. Steele
Ana C. Stephens
Candace Ulmer
Jill Vettrus

Freudenthal Institute Staff

Jan de Lange
Director

Truus Dekker
Coordinator

Mieke Abels
Content Coordinator

Monica Wijers
Content Coordinator

Arthur Bakker
Peter Boon
Els Feijs
Dédé de Haan
Martin Kindt

Nathalie Kuijpers
Huub Nilwik
Sonia Palha
Nanda Querelle
Martin van Reeuwijk

Cover photo credits: (all) © Corbis;

Illustrations
xi (top), **xviii** (bottom) Christine McCabe/ ©Encyclopædia Britannica, Inc.; **1** Holly Cooper-Olds; **1T** Christine McCabe/ ©Encyclopædia Britannica, Inc.; **13** Holly Cooper-Olds; **18, 19** (bottom), **22** Megan Abrams/ © Encyclopædia Britannica, Inc.; **35** Holly Cooper-Olds

Photographs
xvii PhotoDisc/Getty Images; **xviii** (all) Victoria Smith/HRW; **4** Sam Dudgeon/HRW; **7** (middle left) © PhotoDisc/Getty Images; (middle right) © Jack Hollingsworth/PhotoDisc/Getty Images; (bottom) © Corbis; **8** © ImageState; **14** © Stephanie Pilick/AFP/Getty Images; **17** Stephanie Friedman/HRW; **27** John Bortniak, NOAA; **29** © Kenneth Mantai/Visuals Unlimited; **31** (top) Peter Van Steen/HRW Photo; (bottom) CDC; **37** © Corbis; **38** Dynamic Graphics Group/Creatas/Alamy; **39** © Corbis; **43** Victoria Smith/HRW; **44** Sam Dudgeon/HRW Photo; **48** (left to right) © Corbis; © Digital Vision/Getty Images

Contents

Letter to the Teacher

Dear Teacher,

Welcome! *Mathematics in Context* is designed to reflect the National Council of Teachers of *Mathematics Principles and Standards for School Mathematics* and the results of decades of classroom-based education research. *Mathematics in Context* was designed according to principles of Realistic Mathematics Education, a Dutch approach to mathematics teaching and learning where mathematical content is grounded in a variety of realistic contexts to promote student engagement and understanding of mathematics. The term *realistic* is meant to convey that the contexts and mathematics can be made "real in your mind." Rather than relying on you to explain and demonstrate generalized definitions, rules, or algorithms, students investigate questions directly related to a particular context and develop mathematical understanding and meaning from that context.

The curriculum encompasses nine units per grade level. *Ups and Downs* is designed to be the fifth unit in the Algebra strand, but it also lends itself to independent use—to introduce students to experiences that will enrich their understanding for different ways of growth and that will provide students a base to investigate linear and exponential growth in a more formal way in higher grades.

In addition to the teacher guide and student books, *Mathematics in Context* offers the following components that will inform and support your teaching:

- *Teacher Implementation Guide,* which provides an overview of the complete system and resources for program implementation;

- *Number Tools* and *Algebra Tools,* which are black-line master resources that serve as intervention sheets or practice pages to support the development of basic skills and extend student understanding of concepts developed in number and algebra units; and

- *Mathematics in Context Online,* which is a rich, balanced resource for teachers, students, and parents looking for additional information, activities, tools, and support to further students' mathematical understanding and achievements.

Thank you for choosing *Mathematics in Context*. We wish you success and inspiration!

Sincerely,

The Mathematics in Context Development Team

Ups and Downs and the NCTM Principles and Standards for School Mathematics for Grades 6-8

The process standards of Problem Solving, Reasoning and Proof, Communication, Connections, and Representation are addressed across all *Mathematics in Context* units.

In addition, this unit specifically addresses the following PSSM content standards and expectations:

Algebra

In grades 6–8 all students should:

- represent, analyze, and generalize a variety of patterns with tables, graphs, words, and, when possible, symbolic rules;
- relate and compare different forms of representation for a relationship;
- identify functions as linear or nonlinear and contrast their properties from tables, graphs, or equations.
- develop an initial conceptual understanding of different uses of variables;
- explore relationships between symbolic expressions and graphs of lines, paying particular attention to the meaning of *intercept* and *slope*;
- use symbolic algebra to represent situations and to solve problems, especially those that involve linear relationships;
- recognize and generate equivalent forms for simple algebraic expressions and solve linear equations
- model and solve contextualized problems using various representations, such as graphs, tables, and equations; and.
- use graphs to analyze the nature of changes in quantities in linear relationships.

Geometry

In grades 6–8 all students should:

- use geometric models to represent and explain numerical and algebraic relationships; and
- understand relationships among the side lengths and areas of similar objects.

Measurement

In grades 6–8 all students should:

- select and apply techniques and tools to accurately find length and area measures to appropriate levels of precision;
- develop and use formulas to determine the area of circles; and
- solve problems involving scale factors, using ratio and proportion.

Math in the Unit

Prior Knowledge

This unit assumes that students have an understanding of how to:

- use metric measurements;
- create a graph from data in a table;
- find information from a graph;
- describe relationships with direct (word) formulas and NEXT-CURRENT formulas (developed in MiC algebra units *Expressions and Formulas* and *Building Formulas*); and
- relate decimals, fractions, and percents.

Unit Focus

In *Ups and Downs*, students graph, describe, and analyze real data about natural phenomena, including data about plant and human growth.

More formal mathematical language is used to describe changes in growth. Students are introduced to recursive and direct formulas as tools for investigating linear growth. Additional problems about motorcycle rentals reinforce students' understanding of linear growth and prepare them for the concepts of slope and intercept, which are made explicit in the unit *Graphing Equations.*

Year	1	2	3	4	5
Radius (in mm)	4	8	12	16	20

+4 +4 +4 +4

Students investigate linear and quadratic growth by looking at the tables, graphs, and formulas that represent different types of growth. The relationship between the different representations is stressed.

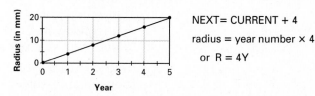

Core Sample of a Tree

NEXT = CURRENT + 4

radius = year number × 4

or R = 4Y

Situations showing linear growth deal with equal increases over equal time periods: the first differences in the table are equal. The graph also shows equal increases over equal time periods: the graph is a straight line.

Length of Square (in cm)	1	2	3	4	5	6
Surface Area of Square (in cm²)	1	4	9	16	25	36

+3 +5 +7 +9 +11

+2 +2 +2 +2

For quadratic relationships, the first differences are not equal, but the second differences are. In the unit *Patterns and Figures,* the concept of first and second differences is reviewed.

Students are informally introduced to exponential growth as they examine the growth patterns of bacteria and weeds. Exponential growth can be modeled with repeated multiplication, the *growth factor* is the ratio between the two numbers for adjoining time periods.

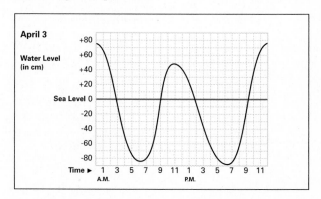

Over the course of the unit, students gain an understanding of periodic functions by looking at such things as the rise and fall of tides, changes in blood pressure with heartbeats, and the speed of a car on a racetrack. Exponential decay is addressed within the context of the absorption of medicine in the blood stream.

When students have finished the unit they will;

- understand formal relationships between different representations like description in words, table, equation, and graph.
  - Students use more formal mathematical language to describe patterns, like *constant rate of change, increasing more and more,* and *growth factor.*
  - Students understand and use recursive and direct formulas.

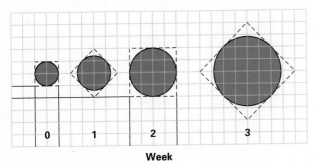

Week

- discern different types of graphs;
  - Line graphs representing information occurring over time, like changes in length of a child, changes in plant growth, and growth of a tree. The graph shows a certain trend but you cannot use one formula or equation to describe it.
  - Straight line, representing a linear function.
  - Periodic graphs.
  - Graphs that show exponential growth or decay.

Body Temperature of a Camel

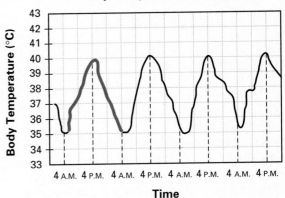

- discern different types of formulas or equations:
  - Equations describing a linear relationship: Rate of change is constant.
  - Equations describing a quadratic relationship: Second differences are equal.
  - Informal use of equations for exponential growth or decay. If each value in the table is found by multiplying by a constant growth factor, the growth is exponential.

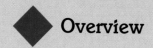
Algebra Strand: An Overview

Mathematical Content

The Algebra strand in *Mathematics in Context* emphasizes algebra as a language used to study relationships among quantities. Students learn to describe these relationships with a variety of representations and to make connections among these representations. The goal is for students to understand the use of algebra as a tool to solve problems that arise in the real world or in the world of mathematics, where symbolic representations can be temporarily freed of meaning to bring a deeper understanding of the problem. Students move from preformal to formal strategies to solve problems, learning to make reasonable choices about which algebraic representation, if any, to use. The goals of the units within the Algebra strand are aligned with NCTM's *Principles and Standards for School Mathematics*.

Algebra Tools and Other Resources

The *Algebra Tools* Workbook provides materials for additional practice and further exploration of algebraic concepts that can be used in conjunction with units in the Algebra strand or independently from individual units. The use of a graphing calculator is optional in the student books. The Teacher's Guides provide additional questions if graphing calculators are used.

Organization of the Algebra Strand

The theme of change and relationships encompasses every unit in the Algebra strand. The strand is organized into three substrands: Patterns and Regularities, Restrictions, and Graphing. Note that units within a substrand are also connected to units in other substrands.

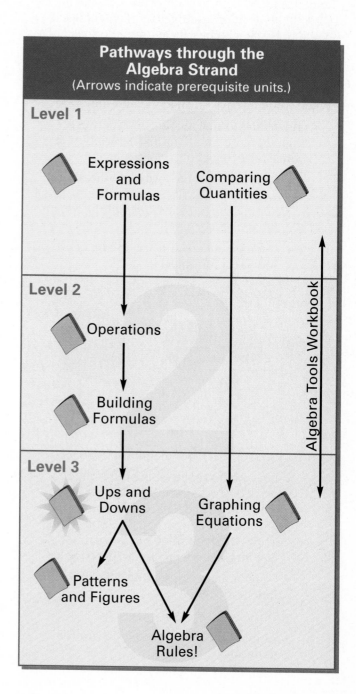

Pathways through the Algebra Strand
(Arrows indicate prerequisite units.)

Level 1
- Expressions and Formulas
- Comparing Quantities

Level 2
- Operations
- Building Formulas

Level 3
- Ups and Downs
- Graphing Equations
- Patterns and Figures
- Algebra Rules!

Algebra Tools Workbook

Patterns and Regularities

In the Patterns and Regularities substrand, students explore and represent patterns to develop an understanding of formulas, equations, and expressions. The first unit, *Expressions and Formulas*, uses arrow language and arithmetic trees to represent situations. With these tools, students create and use word formulas that are the precursors to algebraic equations. The problem below shows how students use arrow language to write and solve equations with a single unknown.

The students use an arrow string to find the height of a stack of cups.

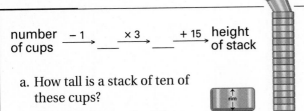

number of cups $\xrightarrow{-1}$ ___ $\xrightarrow{\times 3}$ ___ $\xrightarrow{+15}$ height of stack

a. How tall is a stack of ten of these cups?

b. Explain what each of the numbers in the arrow string represents.

c. These cups need to be stored in a space 50 cm high. How many of these cups can be placed in a stack? Explain how you found your answer.

As problems and calculations become more complicated, students adapt arrow language to include multiplication and division. When dealing with all four arithmetic operations, students learn about the order of operations and use another new tool—arithmetic trees—to help them organize their work and prioritize their calculations. Finally, students begin to generalize their calculations for specific problems using word formulas.

saddle height (in cm) = inseam (in cm) × 1.08
frame height (in cm) = inseam (in cm) × 0.66 + 2

In *Building Formulas*, students explore direct and recursive formulas (formulas in which the current term is used to calculate the next term) to describe patterns. By looking at the repetition of a basic pattern, students are informally introduced to the distributive property. In *Patterns and Figures*, students continue to use and formalize the ideas of direct and recursive formulas and work formally with algebraic expressions, such as $2(n+1)$.

In a recursive (or NEXT-CURRENT) formula, the next number or term in a sequence is found by performing an operation on the current term according to a formula. For many of the sequences in this unit, the next term is a result of adding or subtracting a fixed number from the current term of the sequence. Operations with linear expressions are connected to "Number Strips," or arithmetic sequences.

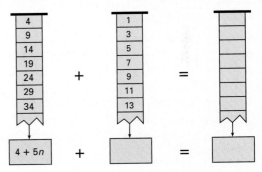

Students learn that they can combine sequences by addition and subtraction. In *Patterns and Figures*, students also encounter or revisit other mathematical topics such as rectangular and triangular numbers. This unit broadens their mathematical experience and makes connections between algebra and geometry.

In the unit *Graphing Equations*, linear equations are solved in an informal and preformal way. The last unit, *Algebra Rules!*, integrates and formalizes the content of algebra substrands. In this unit, a variety of methods to solve linear equations is used in a formal way. Connections to other strands are also formalized. For example, area models of algebraic expressions are used to highlight relationships between symbolic representations and the geometry and measurement strands. In *Algebra Rules!*, students also work with quadratic expressions.

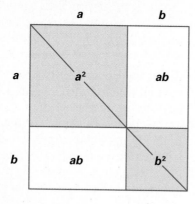

The Patterns and Regularities substrand includes a unit that is closely connected to the Number strand, *Operations*. In this unit, students build on their informal understanding of positive and negative numbers and use these numbers in addition, subtraction, and multiplication. Division of negative numbers is addressed in *Revisiting Numbers* and in *Algebra Rules!*

Restrictions

In the Restrictions substrand, the range of possible solutions to the problems is restricted because the mathematical descriptions of the problem contexts require at least two equations. In *Comparing Quantities*, students explore informal methods for solving systems of equations through nonroutine, yet realistic, problem situations such as running a school store, renting canoes, and ordering in a restaurant.

Within such contexts as bartering, students are introduced to the concept of substitution (exchange) and are encouraged to use symbols to represent problem scenarios. Adding and subtracting relationships graphically and multiplying the values of a graph by a number help students develop a sense of operations with expressions.

To solve problems about the combined costs of varying quantities of such items as pencils and erasers, students use charts to identify possible combinations. They also identify and use the number patterns in these charts to solve problems.

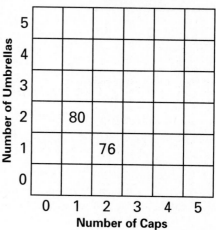

Costs of Combinations (in dollars)

Students' work with problems involving combinations of items is extended as they explore problems about shopping. Given two "picture equations" of different quantities of two items and their combined price, students find the price of a single item. Next, they informally solve problems involving three equations and three variables within the context of a restaurant and the food ordered by people at different tables.

This context also informally introduces matrices. At the end of the unit, students revisit these problem scenarios more formally as they use variables and formal equations to represent and solve problems.

ORDER	TACO	SALAD	DRINK	TOTAL
1	2	4	—	⊕10
2	1	2	3	⊕8
3	3	—	3	⊕9
4	1	2	—	
5	1	—	1	
6	2	2	1	
7	4	2	3	
8				
9				
10				

In *Graphing Equations*, students move from locating points using compass directions and bearings to using graphs and algebraic manipulation to find the point of intersection of two lines.

Students may use graphing calculators to support their work as they move from studying slope to using slope to write equations for lines. Visualizing frogs jumping toward or away from a path helps students develop formal algebraic methods for solving a system of linear equations. In *Algebra Rules!*, the relationship between the point of intersection of two lines (A and B) and the *x*-intercept of the difference between those two lines (A − B) is explored. Students also find that parallel lines relate to a system of equations that have no solution.

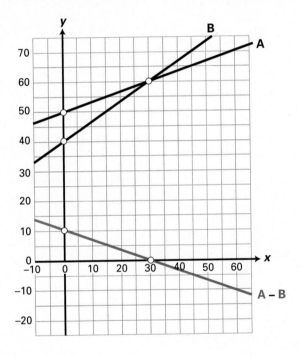

Graphing

The Graphing substrand, which builds on students' experience with graphs in previous number and statistics units, begins with *Expressions and Formulas* where students relate formulas to graphs and read information from a graph.

Operations, which is in the Patterns and Regularities substrand, is also related to the Graphing substrand since it formally introduces the coordinate system.

In *Ups and Downs*, students use equations and graphs to investigate properties of graphs corresponding to a variety of relationships: linear, quadratic, and exponential growth as well as graphs that are periodic.

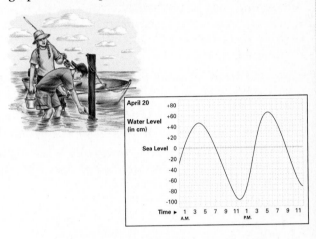

In *Graphing Equations*, students explore the equation of a line in slope and *y*-intercept form. They continuously formalize their knowledge and adopt conventional formal vocabulary and notation, such as origin, quadrant, and *x*-axis, as well as the ordered pairs notation (x, y). In this unit, students use the slope-intercept form of the equation of a line, $y = mx + b$. Students may use graphing calculators to support their work as they move from studying slope to using slope to write equations for lines. Students should now be able to recognize linearity from a graph, a table, and a formula and know the connections between those representations. In the last unit in the Algebra strand, *Algebra Rules!*, these concepts are formalized and the *x*-intercept is introduced. Adding and subtracting relationships graphically and multiplying the values of a graph by a number help students develop a sense of operations with expressions.

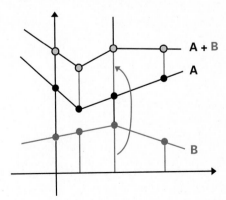

Student Assessment in Mathematics in Context

As recommended by the NCTM *Principles and Standards for School Mathematics* and research on student learning, classroom assessment should be based on evidence drawn from several sources. An assessment plan for a *Mathematics in Context* unit may draw from the following overlapping sources:

- **observation—As students work individually or in groups, watch for evidence of their understanding of the mathematics.**

- **interactive responses—Listen closely to how students respond to your questions and to the responses of other students.**

- **products—Look for clarity and quality of thought in students' solutions to problems completed in class, homework, extensions, projects, quizzes, and tests.**

Assessment Pyramid

When designing a comprehensive assessment program, the assessment tasks used should be distributed across the following three dimensions: mathematics content, levels of reasoning, and difficulty level. The Assessment Pyramid, based on Jan de Lange's theory of assessment, is a model used to suggest how items should be distributed across these three dimensions. Over time, assessment questions should "fill" the pyramid.

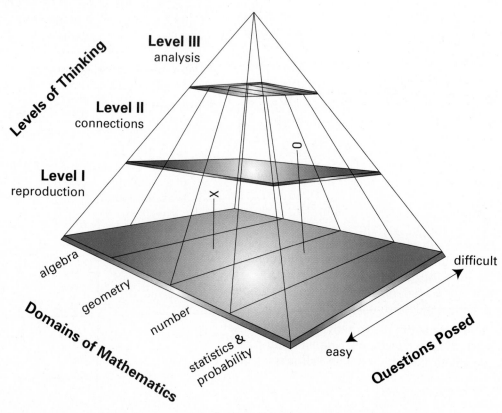

Levels of Reasoning

Level I questions typically address:

- recall of facts and definitions and
- use of technical skills, tools, and standard algorithms.

As shown in the pyramid, Level I questions are not necessarily easy. For example, Level I questions may involve complicated computation problems. In general, Level I questions assess basic knowledge and procedures that may have been emphasized during instruction. The format for this type of question is usually short answer, fill-in, or multiple choice. On a quiz or test, Level I questions closely resemble questions that are regularly found in a given unit substituted with different numbers and/or contexts.

Level II questions require students to:

- integrate information;
- decide which mathematical models or tools to use for a given situation; and
- solve unfamiliar problems in a context, based on the mathematical content of the unit.

Level II questions are typically written to elicit short or extended responses. Students choose their own strategies, use a variety of mathematical models, and explain how they solved a problem.

Level III questions require students to:

- make their own assumptions to solve open-ended problems;
- analyze, interpret, synthesize, reflect; and
- develop one's own strategies or mathematical models.

Level III questions are always open-ended problems. Often, more than one answer is possible, and there is a wide variation in reasoning and explanations. There are limitations to the type of Level III problems that students can be reasonably expected to respond to on time-restricted tests.

The instructional decisions a teacher makes as he or she progresses through a unit may influence the level of reasoning required to solve problems. If a method of problem solving required to solve a Level III problem is repeatedly emphasized during instruction, the level of reasoning required to solve a Level II or III problem may be reduced to recall knowledge, or Level I reasoning. A student who does not master a specific algorithm during a unit but solves a problem correctly using his or her own invented strategy may demonstrate higher-level reasoning than a student who memorizes and applies an algorithm.

The "volume" represented by each level of the Assessment Pyramid serves as a guideline for the distribution of problems and use of score points over the three reasoning levels.

These assessment design principles are used throughout *Mathematics in Context.* The Goals and Assessment charts that highlight ongoing assessment opportunities—on pages xvi and xvii of each Teacher's Guide—are organized according to levels of reasoning.

In the Lesson Notes section of the Teacher's Guide, ongoing assessment opportunities are also shown in the Assessment Pyramid icon located at the bottom of the Notes column.

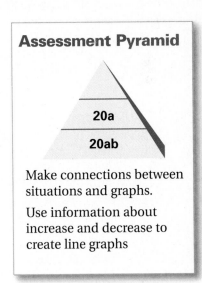

Assessment Pyramid

20a

20ab

Make connections between situations and graphs.

Use information about increase and decrease to create line graphs

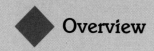

Goals and Assessment

In the *Mathematics in Context* curriculum, unit goals, organized according to levels of reasoning described in the Assessment Pyramid on page xiv, relate to the strand goals and the NCTM Principles and Standards for School Mathematics. The *Mathematics in Context* curriculum is designed to help students demonstrate their understanding of mathematics in each of the categories listed below. Ongoing assessment opportunities are also indicated on their respective pages throughout the Teacher's Guide by an Assessment Pyramid icon.

It is important to note that the attainment of goals in one category is not a prerequisite to the attainment of those in another category. In fact, students should progress simultaneously toward several goals in different categories. The Goals and Assessment table is designed to support preparation of an assessment plan.

	Goal	Ongoing Assessment Opportunities	Unit Assessment Opportunities
Level I: Conceptual and Procedural Knowledge	**1.** Use information about increase and/or decrease to create line graphs.	**Section A** p. 5, #12a p. 6, #13 p. 8, #20b **Section B** p. 15, #4, 7 p. 18, #19	**Quiz 1** #1ad **Test** #1a, 5c
	2. Identify and describe patterns of increase and/or decrease from a table or graph.	**Section A** p. 5, #12ab p. 7, #18 p. 8, #20a **Section B** p. 31, #21	**Quiz 1** #1abc **Quiz 2** #2b **Test** 2abcd, 3abc, 5b
	3. Identify characteristics of periodic graphs.	**Section D** p. 38, #9ab p. 39, #15	**Quiz 2** #2a **Test** #4abc
	4. Identify linear patterns in tables and graphs.	**Section C** p. 24, #4c p. 25, #5c	**Quiz 1** #1c **Test** #3abc, 5bc
	5. Understand and use growth factors.	**Section C** p. 31, #20 **Section E** p. 45, #10	**Quiz 2** #1ac **Test** #5a

	Goal	Ongoing Assessment Opportunities	Unit Assessment Opportunities
Level II: Reasoning, Communicating, Thinking, and Making Connections	**6.** Describe linear, quadratic and exponential growth with recursive formulas.	**Section B** p. 17, #15 **Section C** p. 31, #25 **Section E** p. 45, #11b	**Quiz 2** #1d **Test** #5e
	7. Describe linear growth and direct formulas.	**Section B** p. 18, #20 p. 19, #24a, 25a	**Quiz 1** #2ab **Test** #1b
	8. Make connections between situation, graph, and table.	**Section A** p. 8, #20a **Section E** p. 44, #9	**Quiz 1** #2cd **Quiz 2** #2b **Test** #2d, 3c, 4d, 5bcd
	9. Reason about situations of growth in terms of slope, maximum and minimum, range, decrease and increase.	**Section A** p. 7, #18 **Section B** p. 18, #18 **Section C** p. 28, #14b	**Test** #2d, 5a

	Goal	Ongoing Assessment Opportunities	Unit Assessment Opportunities
Level III: Modeling, Generalizing, and Non-Routine Problem Solving	**10.** Recognize the power of graphs and/or tables for representing and solving problems.	**Section B** p. 19, #26 **Section C** p. 27, #9d	**Test** #5d
	11. Use algebraic models to represent realistic situations.	**Section B** p. 17, #16ab **Section C** p. 24, #3d p. 26, #9b	**Quiz 2** #1b **Test** #5e

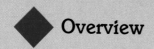

Materials Preparation

The following items are the necessary materials and resources to be used by the teacher and students throughout the unit. For further details, see the Section Overviews and the Materials part of the Hints and Comments section at the top of each teacher page. Note: Some contexts and problems can be enhanced through the use of optional materials. These optional materials are listed in the corresponding Hints and Comments section.

Student Resources

Quantities listed are per student.

• **Letter to the Family**
• **Student Activity Sheets 1–11**

Teacher Resources

No resources required.

Student Materials

Quantities listed are per pair of students, unless otherwise noted.

• **Calculator**
• **Centimeter ruler**
• **Colored pencils, one box**
• **Compass**
• **Graph paper (12 sheets per student)**
• **Scissors**

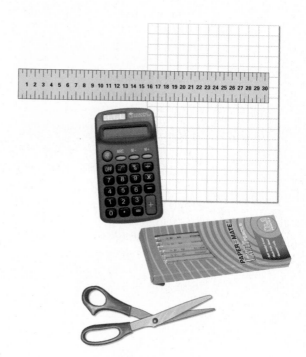

Student Material and Teaching Notes

◆ Contents

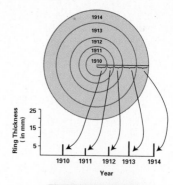

Dear Student,

Welcome to *Ups and Downs*. In this unit, you will look at situations that change over time, such as blood pressure or the tides of an ocean. You will learn to represent these changes using tables, graphs, and formulas.

Graphs of temperatures and tides show up-and-down movement, but some graphs, such as graphs for tree growth or melting ice, show only upward or only downward movement.

As you become more familiar with graphs and the changes that they represent, you will begin to notice and understand graphs in newspapers, magazines, and advertisements.

During the next few weeks, look for graphs and statements about growth, such as "Fast-growing waterweeds in lakes become a problem." Bring to class interesting graphs and newspaper articles and discuss them.

Telling a story with a graph can help you understand the story.

Sincerely,

The Mathematics in Context Development Team

Section Focus

Students investigate growth over time within a variety of contexts using statements (stories), tables, and graphs. They create and use line graphs to represent continuous processes that occur over time. Students describe growth patterns in their own words, using expressions such as "faster and faster" or "increased every week by equal amounts." Lines are used to connect data so that a trend becomes visible. The formal term *linear growth* is used. The instructional focus of Section A is to:

- **identify and describe growth patterns from a story, table, or graph;**
- **create line graphs from data in a table; and**
- **solve problems involving growth patterns.**

Pacing and Planning

Day 1: Wooden Graphs		Student pages 1–4
INTRODUCTION	Problems 1–5	Use tree rings in the cross section of a tree to estimate its age.
CLASSWORK	Problems 6–8	Compare the cross sections of tree stumps to determine their relative age and when they were cut down.
HOMEWORK	Problems 9–11	Interpret a series of marks on a door every year to indicate the height of a person.

Day 2: Growing Up		Student pages 5–7
INTRODUCTION	Review homework.	Review homework from Day 1.
CLASSWORK	Problems 12–17	Graph the weight and length of a baby over the first 36 months of life.
HOMEWORK	Problem 18	Interpret patterns of decrease from a table.

Day 3: Water for the Desert		Student pages 7–12
INTRODUCTION	Review homework.	Review homework from Day 2.
CLASSWORK	Problems 19–23	Match tables, graphs, and stories that describe the growth of sunflowers.
HOMEWORK	Check Your Work	Student self-assessment: Graph and interpret growth patterns.

Additional Resources: *Algebra Tools*; Additional Practice, Section A, pages 47–49

Materials

Student Resources

Quantities listed are per student.

- Letter to the Family
- **Student Activity Sheets 1–4**

Teachers Resources

No resources required.

Student Materials

Quantities listed are per pair of students, unless otherwise noted.

- Centimeter ruler
- Compass
- Graph paper (three sheets per student)
- Scissors

* See Hints and Comments for optional materials.

Learning Lines

Discern Different Types of Graphs

This section focuses on growth patterns, shown in a variety of graphs:

- a diagram of the thickness of rings of a tree;
- a line graph representing a child's growth over a number of years;
- growth curves representing average growth of a child over a number of months;
- a straight line representing linear growth; and
- curved lines, showing a growth pattern that becomes "faster and faster" or "less and less."

Different Representations for A Relationship

Students use tables to identify patterns. They interpret growth patterns by looking at the graph and are introduced to the concept of different rates of increase (or decrease). By relating growth patterns to graphical representations, students recognize the faster the growth, the steeper the graph. They use the tables and graphs to predict future growth and make connections between situation, graph, and table.

At the End of This Section; Learning Outcomes

Students are able to write a story to describe growth patterns in a table or graph, and recognize the power of graphs and/or tables for representing and solving problems. Students begin to identify and describe patterns of increase or decrease and reason about the situations in which they occur.

You may want to have a short class discussion about sequoia trees, focusing on the diameter of the trunks. Ask students whether they have seen or heard of these trees.

1 You may want to briefly discuss the difference between *circumference* and *diameter* after students have revealed their understanding of the two terms.

2 Discuss why the rings, not the lines, need to be counted.

Trendy Graphs

Wooden Graphs

Giant sequoia trees grow in Sequoia National Park in California. The largest tree in the park is thought to be between 3,000 and 4,000 years old.

It takes 16 children holding hands to reach around the giant sequoia shown here.

1. Find a way to estimate the circumference and diameter of this tree.

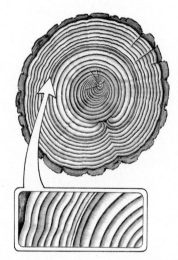

This is a drawing of a cross section of a tree. Notice its distinct ring pattern. The bark is the dark part on the outside. During each year of growth, a new layer of cells is added to the older wood. Each layer forms a ring. The distance between the dark rings shows how much the tree grew that year.

2. Look at the cross section of the tree. Estimate the age of this tree. How did you find your answer?

Take a closer look at the cross section. The picture below the cross section shows a magnified portion.

3. a. Looking at the magnified portion, how can you tell that this tree did not grow the same amount each year?

b. Reflect What are some possible reasons for the tree's uneven growth?

Reaching All Learners

Intervention

Students who count 16 years are referring to the magnified portion of the tree rings and should be redirected to count the rings in the complete cross section. If students have difficulty seeing that they need to count the rings and not the lines, you might ask students to draw a cross section of a tree with four rings and then color one of the rings.

Act It Out

After solving the problem, have a group of 16 students form a circle with their arms extended out to the sides so that they can get a better sense of the magnitude of the circumference of this tree.

Solutions and Samples

1. Estimates and strategies will vary. Sample response:

   When you hold your arms out horizontally, the distance between the fingertips of your left and right hands is approximately the same as your height, measured from head to toe.

   If you assume that these children are about 1.5 m tall, then the circumference will be about 16 × 1.5 = 24 m. Use the relationship between circumference and diameter. The diameter can be found by calculating 24m ÷ π = 7.6 m.

2. Sample response:

   About 26 or 27 years. I found my answer by counting the rings.

3. **a.** Some students may say that the rings have different widths.

   b. Sample responses:
   - lack of water
   - a long, cold winter
   - a spring frost
   - a disease

Hints and Comments

Materials

centimeter rulers (one per student); paper strips, (optional, one per group of students); measuring tape (optional, one per group of students)

Overview

Students estimate the circumference and diameter of a giant sequoia tree shown in the picture on Student Book page 1. They use a cross section of a tree to estimate the age of the tree.

About the Mathematics

To solve problem 1, students can use the experiences and knowledge they have acquired in previous units or in previous grades.

- A person's arm span measures about the same as his or her height. The historic word for arm span is *fathom*.

- The diameter is the length of a straight line through the center of a circle. The circumference is the perimeter of a circle. These concepts were introduced in the unit *Reallotment*.

- Sizes of pictured objects can be estimated using the standard sizes of familiar things that appear near the object in question.

- The constancy of the ratio between circumference and diameter is a bit more than three (some students may remember it as pi, π). This is one of the concepts studied in *Reallotment*.

Looking at the thickness of the rings of a cross section of a tree shows how much the radius of the tree increased each year. The study of the thickness of the rings will develop students' understanding of different rates of increase, which is one of the main topics of this unit.

Comments About the Solutions

1. To suggest the relationship between arm span and height, you may want to reference Leonardo da Vinci's 1492 sketch, *Vitruvian Man*.

A Trendy Graphs

Notes

It is important that students know that rings grow on the outside rather than from the inside.

Tree growth is directly related to the amount of moisture supplied. Look at the cross section on page 1 again. Notice that one of the rings is very narrow.

4. a. What conclusion can you draw about the rainfall during the year that produced the narrow ring?

   b. How old was the tree that year?

The oldest known living tree is a bristlecone pine (*Pinus aristata*) named Methuselah. Methuselah is about 4,700 years old and grows in the White Mountains of California.

It isn't necessary to cut down a tree in order to examine the pattern of rings. Scientists use a technique called **coring** to take a look at the rings of a living tree. They use a special drill to remove a piece of wood from the center of the tree. This piece of wood is about the thickness of a drinking straw and is called a *core sample*. The growth rings show up as lines on the core sample.

By matching the ring patterns from a living tree with those of ancient trees, scientists can create a calendar of tree growth in a certain area.

The picture below shows how two core samples are matched up. Core sample B is from a living tree. Core sample A is from a tree that was cut down in the same area. Matching the two samples in this way produces a "calendar" of wood.

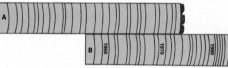

5 As a hint, discuss whether you can match up any one year easily. (The thinnest ring is easiest to see on both trees.)

5. In what year was the tree represented by core sample A cut down?

Reaching All Learners

Extension

Ask one student to bring in a cross section of a tree to count rings with the rest of the class.

Solutions and Samples

4. a. Sample response:

The tree didn't grow very much that year, so perhaps there was not much rain.

b. The tree was about 19 years old.

5. 1973

Hints and Comments

Overview

Students use a cross section of a tree to estimate the age of the tree and to draw conclusions about the tree's growth. They learn how rings of living trees can be investigated by taking a core sample. They read about the strategy of matching core samples to create a calendar of tree growth.

Planning

Students may work in pairs or small groups on problems 3–5. After they finish these problems, you might have a short class discussion on the meaning of the thickness of the rings. Be sure students understand why it is possible to compare the core samples taken from different trees by matching the lines.

A Trendy Graphs

Notes

Ask students how they would figure out what period of time sample C would represent.

6 Have students shade every tenth year for ease in counting.

Have students cut out only sample C and then match it to samples A and B.

The next picture shows a core sample from another tree that was cut down. If you match this one to the other samples, the calendar becomes even longer. Enlarged versions of the three strips can be found on **Student Activity Sheet 1**.

6. What period of time is represented by the three core samples?

Instead of working with the actual core samples or drawings of core samples, scientists transfer the information from the core samples onto a diagram like this one.

7. About how thick was the ring in 1910?

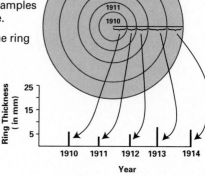

Totem Pole

Tracy found a totem pole in the woods behind her house. It had fallen over, so Tracy could see the growth rings on the bottom of the pole. She wondered when the tree from which it was made was cut down.

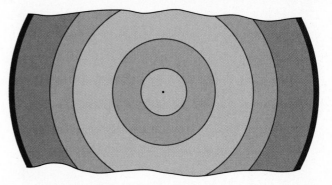

Reaching All Learners

Intervention

Suggest that students look for similar patterns in samples B and C and line them up. As a hint, ask students if they can match up any one year easily. (The thinnest ring is the easiest to see.)

Solutions and Samples

6. The period of time represented by the samples is from 1919 to 1994.

This is the way the patterns match. Note: Each dot marks the beginning of a new decade.

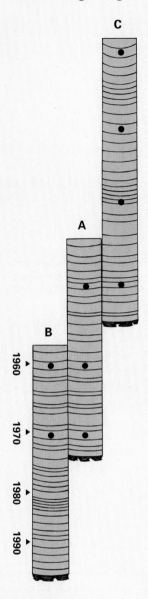

7. About six millimeters (mm) or 0.6 centimeters (cm). Accept answers between five and seven mm.

Hints and Comments

Materials

Student Activity Sheet 1 (one per student); scissors (one pair per student)

Overview

Students match three core samples in order to find out what period of time the calendar of wood represents.

About the Mathematics

A diagram that shows the annual increase in the radius of a tree can be used to reconstruct the cross section of the tree. The diagram also can be used to construct a graph that shows the total radius of the tree over time. Note that if you want to have a graph that shows the growth of the diameter over time, you can double the measurements of the radius to get the diameter.

Planning

Students may work on problems 6 and 7 in pairs or small groups. After students finish the problems, you may want to discuss them in class. After you discuss problem 6 in class, ask students to describe the connection between the tree rings and the diagram. This connection is investigated further on the next page.

Notes

You may want to introduce the context about Marsha's growth by talking about similarities between this and the previous context. Ask students questions like, *What is the average height of a door? Does a child grow with the same rate of change every year? What is the average length of a baby after its birth* (in American measurements as well as centimeters)? *How do the core samples and the door marks relate?*

9–11 Check and discuss students' solutions for problems 9–11.

Tracy asked her friend Luis, who studies plants and trees in college, if he could help her find the age of the wood. He gave her the diagram pictured below, which shows how cedar trees that were used to make totem poles grew in their area.

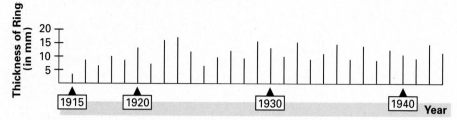

8. a. Make a similar diagram of the thickness of the rings of the totem pole that Tracy found.

  b. Using the diagram above, can you find the age of the totem pole? What year was the tree cut down?

Growing Up

On Marsha's birthday, her father marked her height on her bedroom door. He did this every year from her first birthday until she was 19 years old.

  9. There are only 16 marks. Can you explain this?

  10. How old was Marsha when her growth slowed considerably?

  11. Where would you put a mark to show Marsha's height at birth?

Reaching All Learners

Intervention

If students are having difficulties, refer them to the drawing in problem 7 on the previous page to review how a diagram can be constructed from a cross section.

Extension

Have students find various designs for totem poles on the Internet.

Solutions and Samples

8. a.

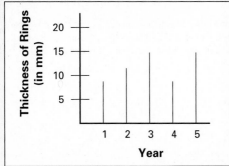

Note: This diagram shows differences in growth from one year to the next. These differences are not equal. In the next section, where we look at linear patterns, the differences from one step to the next are equal.

b. The graph matches the period from 1933 to 1937 in Luis's diagram, so the tree was cut down in 1937, and the totem pole was made sometime after that. Assuming that 2005 is the current year, the totem pole would be about 68 years old.

9. She stopped growing at age 16. Another less likely reason is that she stopped growing from one year to the next.

10. Answers will vary. Some students may say age 13 because her growth slowed when she was 13 (the growth from age 13 to age 14 is less than age 12 to age 13). Other students may say age 14 because she grew half the amount of the year before, and the marks after age 14 are very close.

11. Answers will vary. A good estimate would be about halfway between the floor and the first mark. Some students may use their own birth length as an estimate. Many newborns average 55 cm, or 21 in., in length. All students should see that the newborn mark should at least be below the 1-year mark.

Hints and Comments

Materials

millimeter graph paper (optional, one sheet per student);
centimeter rulers (one per student)

Overview

Students use a diagram to date a wooden totem pole. They interpret marks that are put on a door every year to indicate the height of a person.

About the Mathematics

The marks on the door are similar to the core sample of a tree: the distances between the lines show the yearly increase, or the rate of growth per year.

Planning

Students may work in pairs or in small groups on problem 8.

Comments About the Problems

8. a. Observe students measuring the thickness of the rings in millimeters. Students should know that if they want to measure the thickness of the rings precisely, they have to measure along the diameter of the circle. Students may want to use graph paper for drawing the diagram.

b. Wood is usually allowed to dry a few years before it is carved. So the totem could have been made as early as 1937 but probably was made sometime after that year.

11. One way to think about this problem is to use the doorknob as a point of reference. A doorknob is about 1 m from the floor. Imagine that a newborn baby would be about half that length, or 50 cm. So you would put a mark halfway between the doorknob and the floor.

A ◆ Trendy Graphs

Notes

This problem is critical because it is the first time in the unit that students construct a graph.

Be sure to relate the marks on the door, shown on the left margin of the graph, to the scale on the vertical axis.

When students have finished, draw the graph of Marsha's growth on a transparency and discuss these problems in class. Students should realize that it is easier to project a growth pattern forward or backward in time when you have a graph.

Whenever something is graphed "over time," the variable representing time should be placed on the horizontal axis.

12. a. Use **Student Activity Sheet 2** to draw a graph of Marsha's growth. Use the marks on the door to get the vertical coordinates. Marsha's height was 52 centimeters (cm) at birth.

b. How does the graph show that Marsha's growth slowed down at a certain age?

c. How does the graph show the year during which she had her biggest growth spurt?

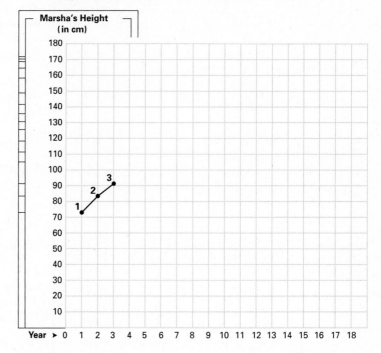

The graph you made for problem 12 is called a **line graph** or plot over time. It represents information occurring over time. If you connect the ends of the segments of the graph you made for problem 8 on page 4, you would also see a plot over time of the differences in growth of the tree from one year to the next. These graphs show a certain trend, like how Marsha has grown or how the tree grew each year. You cannot write one formula or equation to describe the growth.

Assessment Pyramid

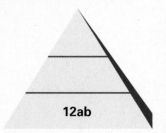

12ab

Use information about increase to create line graphs.

Reaching All Learners

Intervention

You might need to point out to students that the points marked "1," "2," and "3" on the graph represent years of age

Parent Involvement

Have students find their birth length and height on a birth certificate or other similar records. Have them work with their parents to make a graph of their heights at select ages (from medical records or door markings). If their height information is not readily available, encourage them to make reasonable estimates.

Solutions and Samples

12. a. Sample graph:

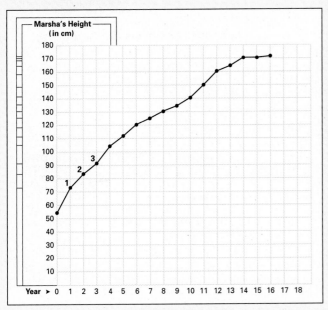

Marsha's Height (in cm)

b. The graph starts to level off (starting at age 12). Before that, the graph rises steadily.

c. The biggest growth spurt occurs where the graph rises most sharply (which is between ages zero and one).

Hints and Comments

Materials

Student Activity Sheet 2 (one per student); transparency of **Student Activity Sheet 2**, (optional, one per class); overhead projector (optional, one per class)

Overview

Students use the marks on the door to create a graph that shows a person's height over time.

About the Mathematics

Line graphs are created to show how a person's height grows over time. This graph can be used to make connections between the differences in growth. For example, a larger distance between two marks on the door indicates a growth spurt during that period, and the graph for that period is, therefore, steeper. The steepness of a curve over a given period of time lays the foundation for the study of rate of change in calculus.

The dots of a *line graph* may be connected by a smooth line if the information is derived from numbers that are continuous, as depth of water at low/high tide, etc. A continuous graph does not have "holes" of missing data. If the information is *discrete* as in snapshots of the time at which runners pass a reference point during a race, the dots should not be represented by a continuous graph. However, the dots are sometimes connected by small straight lines to show a *trend*. These straight lines have no meaning in themselves.

Planning

Students may work individually on problem 12. You might discuss problem 12 focusing on the relationship between the positions of the marks on the door and the steepness of the graph.

A Trendy Graphs

Notes

13 You might have students discuss which answers are reasonable. Discuss the average weight and length of a newborn child in customary and metric units.

The curves in the charts show the results of measurements of the weights and lengths of a group of young boys. The dark line in the center of each set of lines is the median weight or height for boys, or the fiftieth percentile. The bands show the distribution of the middle 90% of children, from the fifth to the ninety-fifth percentile.

Ask students, *Is "age" on the horizontal axis of the growth charts for a reason?* (Yes, it represents time.)

Growth Charts

Healthcare workers use growth charts to help monitor the growth of children up to age three.

13. Why is it important to monitor a child's growth?

The growth chart below shows the weight records, in kilograms (kg), of a 28-month-old boy.

Month	Birth	1	2	3	4	5	6	7	8	9	10	11	12	13	14	15
Weight	2.7	3.6	5.7	7.0	7.3	7.8	8.0	8.8	8.8	8.8	9.3	9.6	10.5	10.3	11.3	12.0
Month	16	17	18	19	20	21	22	23	24	25	26	27	28			
Weight	12.4	12.9	13.1	12.9	10.5	9.2	9.5	12.0	13.0	13.6	13.5	14.0	14.2			

14. What conclusion can you draw from this table? Do you think this boy gained weight in a "normal" way?

The graphs that follow show normal ranges for the weights and heights of young children in one country. The normal growth range is indicated by curved lines.

Note: The zigzag line on the lower left of the height graph indicates that the lower part of the graph, from 0–40, is omitted.

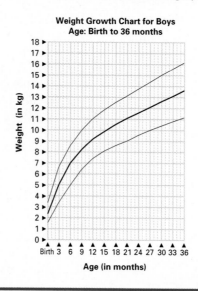

Weight Growth Chart for Boys
Age: Birth to 36 months

Height Growth Chart for Boys
Age: Birth to 36 months

© Am. J. Nutr.
American Society for Clinical Nutrition

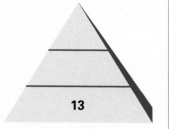
Reaching All Learners

Accommodation

The tables and graphs on this page are in metric to motivate students to make connections between the metric system and measurement units that they are more familiar with, for example, inches, feet, and pounds. Some reference points that could be discussed are: 10 kg is about 22 lb; 100 cm is a bit more than 3 ft. If students have difficulty relating the two, the table values and scales on the growth charts could be rewritten using inches and pounds.

Solutions and Samples

13. Sample responses:
- To make sure the child is healthy.
- A healthy child should grow and gain weight.
- To make sure the child is eating properly.
- If the child weighs too little, it is not healthy.

14. Sample response:

The boy seemed to be gaining weight and growing until he was 18 months old. From 18 to 22 months old, he lost weight. Then from 22 months old to 28 months old, he started gaining weight again.

Hints and Comments

Materials

transparencies of the charts on Student Book page 6 (optional, one per class);
overhead projector (optional, one per class)

Overview

Students investigate a weight growth chart and a length growth chart. They compare "normal" growth to the actual measurements of problem 13. They investigate a table showing weight records for a young child from birth up to the age of 28 months.

About the Mathematics

All growth situations in the preceding problems showed increases in height, size, or some other measurement. On this page, decrease is introduced in the form of weight loss. Using the records in the table, one can distinguish increase from decrease by using positive and negative numbers for these differences:

Month	Weight (in kg)	
11	9.6	) + 0.9
12	10.5	) − 0.2
13	10.3	) + 1.0
14	11.3	

Planning

You may want to make transparencies of the growth charts and use them to lead a class discussion of trends in human growth.

Notes

17a You might point out that most babies are not weighed every month.

18 During the discussion of student answers, you may want to point out that the seriousness of the weight loss might depend on the child's height.

15. Describe how the growth of a "normal" boy changes from birth until the age of three.

In both graphs, one curved line is thicker than the other two.

16. **a.** What do these thicker curves indicate?

   b. These charts are for boys. How do you think charts for girls would differ from these?

17. **a.** Graph the weight records from problem 13 on the weight growth chart on **Student Activity Sheet 3**.

   b. Study the graph that you made. What conclusions can you draw from the graph?

Here are four weekly weight records for two children. The records began when the children were one year old.

	Week 1	Week 2	Week 3	Week 4
Samantha's Weight (in kg)	11.8	11.6	11.3	10.9
Hillary's Weight (in kg)	10.5	10.0	9.7	9.5

18. Although both children are losing weight, which one would you worry about more? Why?

Water for the Desert

In many parts of the world, you can find deserts near the sea. Because there is a water shortage in the desert, you might think that you could use the nearby sea as a water source. Unfortunately, seawater contains salt that would kill the desert plants.

Assessment Pyramid

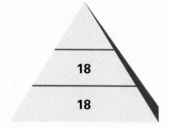

18

18

Reason about situations of growth in terms of slope, range, increase, and decrease.

Identify patterns in graphs.

Reaching All Learners

Intervention

Before having students complete the graph in 17a, have student volunteers model on an overhead transparency how to estimate the plotting of decimal values on the growth chart.

Vocabulary Building

During class discussion of the growth chart, have some students share their definitions for *mean* and *median*. Some students might remember these terms from the unit *Dealing with Data*.

Solutions and Samples

15. Sample response: During the first six months, a "normal" boy grows fast. After six months, the rate of change differs; the growth slows down. After one year, the growth rate slows down again but less than after six months. From 12 months until age three, the rate of change is almost constant; the boy grows steadily but not as fast as the previous period.

16. a. The thicker curves show the median weights and heights for boys. Half of the boys are heavier or taller than the thick line, and half are lighter or shorter.

   b. Sample response: Girls are usually shorter at birth and lighter than boys. The graphs for girls will start at a lower number and will be more or less parallel to the boys' graphs.

17. a.

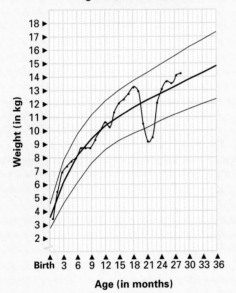

Weight Growth Chart for Boys
Age: Birth to 36 months

Weight (in kg) — 18, 17, 16, 15, 14, 13, 12, 11, 10, 9, 8, 7, 6, 5, 4, 3, 2

Age (in months) — Birth, 3, 6, 9, 12, 15, 18, 21, 24, 27, 30, 33, 36

   b. Sample response: The baby's weight gain was normal until he was 18 months old. At this point he lost weight very fast. Three months later, he gained the weight back almost as fast. After that point he seemed to gain weight normally.

18. Sample responses:

   • I would worry about Samantha because she loses more weight each week than the week before, so she is getting worse all of the time.

   • I would worry more about Hillary because she weighs the least.

   • I would not worry as much about Hillary as Samantha because Hillary lost a lot at first but now is only losing a little bit, so her loss is slowing down.

Hints and Comments

Materials

Student Activity Sheet 3, one per student.

Overview

Students investigate the weight records of two children, presented in two tables. They are then introduced to problems in a new context, icebergs as a source of fresh water.

About the Mathematics

Focus on increase and/or decrease in a situation about growth.

Comments About the Problems

18. Samantha's weight loss could be considered more serious because it is more each week than the week before. Hillary's weight loss could be more serious because she weighs less than Samantha.

A Trendy Graphs

Notes

Some scientists are investigating ways to bring ice from the Antarctic Ocean to the desert. The ice from an iceberg is made from fresh water. It is well packed and can be easily pulled by boat. However, there is one problem: The ice would melt during the trip, and the water from the melted ice would be lost.

There are different opinions about how the iceberg might melt during a trip. The three graphs illustrate different opinions.

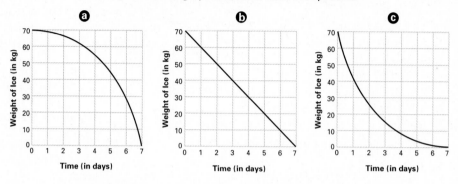

The graphs are not based on data, but they show possible trends.

19. **Reflect** Use the graphs to describe, in your own words, what the three opinions are.

19 Discuss students' answers to this problem in class. It will be helpful for students to hear how other students describe the graphs.

Sunflowers

Roxanne, Jamal, and Leslie did a group project on sunflower growth for their biology class. They investigated how different growing conditions affect plant growth. Each student chose a different growing condition.

The students collected data every week for five weeks. At the end of the five weeks, they were supposed to write a group report that would include a graph and a story for each of three growing conditions.

Unfortunately, when the students put their work together, the pages were scattered, and some were lost. The graphs and written reports that were left are shown on the next page.

20. a. Find which graph and written report belong to each student.

b. Create the missing graph.

20a and **b** You may find it helpful to copy and cut out each of the notes and have students reorganize them and paste them on a sheet of paper.

Assessment Pyramid

Make connections between situations and graphs.

Use information about increase and decrease to create line graphs.

Reaching All Learners

Intervention

If students have difficulty completing this problem, be sure to give extra attention to different possible patterns of increase and decrease when discussing the section Summary on page 10.

Extension

Over the course of a school day, conduct an ongoing experiment to collect data on the rate at which ice melts. Take weight measurements of the ice every 20 minutes. Use different conditions: the shape of the ice (with the same volume), wind (fan blowing), climate (different locations around the room), etc. Revisit the data and graphs for each condition the next day and compare to the graphs for problem 19.

Solutions and Samples

19. Descriptions will vary. Sample responses:

Graph **a** shows a situation in which every day there will be more of the volume melting than the day before. Or the ice is melting quicker and quicker.

In graph **b**, the volume decreases by the same amount every day. Or the rate of change of the decrease is constant.

Graph **c** shows that every day there is less ice melting than the day before. Or the ice is melting slower and slower.

20. a. Roxanne's report (**a**) belongs to graph **d**; Leslie's report (**c**) belongs to graph **b**; Jamal's graph is missing.

b. Sample table and graph for Jamal. Students' graphs may be different.

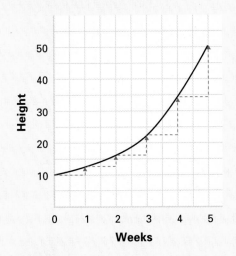

Weeks	0	1	2	3	4	5
Height	10	12	17	23	35	50

+2   +5   +6   +12   +15

Hints and Comments

Overview

Students explain graphs that show different opinions about ways an iceberg might melt. They are introduced to a new context, growing sunflowers.

About the Mathematics

The rate at which an iceberg melts may depend on different circumstances: the temperature of air and water, the wind, the movement of the water, and the shape and size of the iceberg. The shape of the iceberg is quite important. A flat iceberg would melt more quickly than an iceberg with the same volume but in the shape of a sphere (or a cube) because its surface area is greater. This can be shown by comparing a block and a cube with the same volume as shown below.

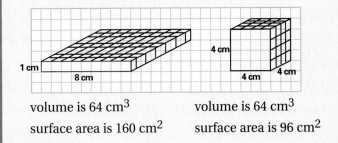

volume is 64 cm^3 volume is 64 cm^3

surface area is 160 cm^2 surface area is 96 cm^2

Planning

Students may work individually on problem 19. You may want to assign the problem as homework.

22b Clarify that all tables are not ratio tables. In a ratio table the ratio between the two values must be the same. Discuss examples in the "About the Mathematics" section on page 9T with students.

23b You may want to discuss the concept of a *constant rate of change*, which occurs if growth is linear.

The type of growth displayed by Roxanne's sunflower is called **linear growth**.

21. Why do you think it is called linear growth?

A plant will hardly ever grow in a linear way all the time, but for some period, the growth might be linear. Consider a sunflower that has a height of 20 cm when you start your observation and grows 1.5 cm per day.

22. a. In your notebook, copy and fill in the table.

Time (in days)	0	1	2	3	4	5	6	7	8
Height (in cm)	20	21.5							

b. Meryem thinks this is a ratio table. Is she right? Explain your answer.

c. How does the table show linear growth?

d. Use your table to draw a graph. Use the vertical axis for height (in centimeters) and the horizontal axis for time (in days). Label the axes.

Here is a table with data from another sunflower growth experiment.

Time (in weeks)	0	1	2	3	4	5	6
Height (in cm)	10	12.5	17.5	25	35	47.5	

23. a. How can you be sure that the growth during this period was not linear?

b. In your own words, describe the growth of this plant.

Reaching All Learners

Advanced Learners

Have students make up six tables: three that are ratio tables and three that are not ratio tables. Have them explain the difference between the two sets of tables. You may also have students graph each table to have them discover a distinctive feature of graphs for ratio tables. They are linear graphs that intersect the origin (0, 0).

Vocabulary Building

After completing the Sunflowers activity, have students include a definition for linear growth in their notebooks. With their definition, have students include an example of linear growth represented in a table and a graph.

Solutions and Samples

21. Sample answers:

- I think the growth is called linear because the graph is a straight line.

- I think the growth is called linear because the length increased each week by equal amounts.

22. a.

Time (in days)	0	1	2	3	4	5	6	7	8
Height (in cm)	20	21.5	23	24.5	26	27.5	29	30.5	32

b. No, this is not a ratio table. The ratio between time and height changes throughout the table. The ratio 2 to 23 is about 1:11, but the ratio 8 to 32 is 1:4.

c. Each day, the sunflower grows 1.5 cm. The rate of change in the height for each day is constant.

d. Graph:

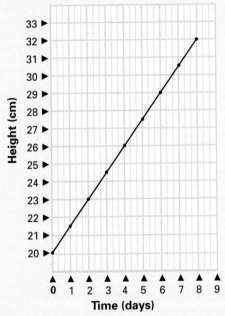

23. a. The height of the sunflower increases by 2.5, 5, 7.5, 10, and 12.5 cm, which are not equal amounts. Or the rate of change in the second row of the table is not constant.

b. At the start of the experiment, the sunflower did not grow very fast, but it started to grow faster soon. After 3 weeks, its height was already 2.5 times the original height.

Note: Have students look at the rate of change. This is not constant, but the differences in the rates of change are constant (2.5 cm).

Hints and Comments

Overview

Students match graphs and stories, and recreate the missing graph.

About the Mathematics

Some students may think that these kinds of tables are always ratio tables. An explanation of how to tell whether or not a table is a ratio table follows.

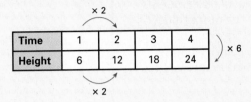

This table is a ratio table because the ratio between time and height is 1:6. In other words, if you double (triple, etc.) the time, then you get double (triple, etc.) the height. The graph that corresponds to this table is a straight line (starting at the origin).

The relationship between the numbers in the following table is different:

Time	1	2	3	4
Height	15	20	25	30

This is not a ratio table. The graph is a straight line, but it doesn't start at the origin. Linear growth patterns are investigated further in Section B of this unit. This problem is an introduction to that section.

Planning

Students may work in pairs or in small groups on problems 21–23.

Notes

The Summary for this section reiterates each of the strategies used in the section. Go through the Summary carefully, having students read parts aloud. It is critical that students review the terminology used to describe patterns of increase and decrease presented in this section.

 Trendy Graphs

Summary

Information about growth over time can be obtained by looking at:

- a statement like "My sunflower grew faster and faster."
- growth "calendars" like the tree rings appearing on a core sample or the height marks made on a door.
- tables like the growth charts used for babies.
- line graphs. The line graphs used in this section show trends.

You can draw a graph by using the information in a table. Often, the graph will give more information than the table.

By looking at a graph, you can see whether and how something is increasing or decreasing over time.

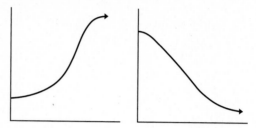

The shape of a graph shows how a value increases or decreases. The following graph and table show a value that is decreasing more and more.

Days	0	1	2	3
Weight	25	23	19	10

−2   −4   −9

Reaching All Learners

Parent Involvement

Have parents review the section with their child to relate the Check Your Work problems to the problems from the section.

Extension

During the discussion of the Summary, you might say, *Tracy looked at the first graph on the left and said, "It's increasing at first but decreasing towards the end."* Ask students whether they agree or disagree with Tracy and explain why. (The graph is still increasing toward the end, but it is increasing more slowly.) You might ask a similar question for the graph on the right.

Hints and Comments

Overview

In the Summary, students review how information about growth over time can be obtained in different ways: by looking at statements, graphs, tables, core samples of a tree, or marks on a door post. They see how the shape of a graph shows that the value decreases more and more rapidly over time.

About the Mathematics

When the pattern of increase or decrease is investigated, it is important that the differences be calculated for equal time intervals and that the same time intervals are used in corresponding tables and graphs.

The dotted lines in the graph at the bottom of the Summary show these time intervals, and the arrows show the differences.

Another way to display the differences is by the following diagram.

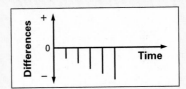

The lines in the diagram are related to the arrows on the graph in the Summary, and they point downward to indicate decreasing values. Although this type of diagram was useful at the beginning of this section because it represented real-world situations, using it here is probably too abstract for students to understand.

Notes

Be sure to go over the Check Your Work problems with students so that they learn whether their answer is correct, even if it does not exactly match the answer given.

1a If students are having difficulty drawing circles or measuring distances with a compass, you may want to demonstrate the proper techniques of drawing and measuring with compasses on the board or overhead.

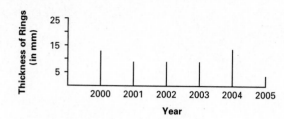

This diagram represents the thickness of annual rings of a tree. It shows how much the tree grew each year.

1. a. Use a ruler and a compass to draw a cross section of this tree. The first two rings are shown here. Copy and continue this drawing to show the complete cross section.

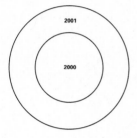

b. Write a story that describes how the tree grew.

This table shows Dean's growth.

Age (in years)	1	2	3	4	5	6	7	8	9	10	11	12	13	14	15	16	17	18
Height (in cm)	80	95	103	109	114	118	124	130	138	144	150	156	161	170	176	181	185	187

2. a. Draw a line graph of Dean's height on **Student Activity Sheet 4**.

b. What does this graph show that is not easy to see in the table?

c. At what age did Dean have his biggest growth spurt?

Assessment Pyramid

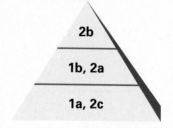

2b

1b, 2a

1a, 2c

Assesses Section A Goals

Reaching All Learners

Parent Involvement

Students should share their work on these problems with their parents. Students should be able to show their parents which strategies they used for each problem.

Solutions and Samples

Answers to Check Your Work

1. a. Note: The figure is not drawn to scale.

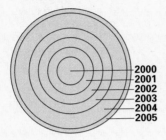

b. Your story may differ from the two sample stories below.

First it was planted. It got plenty of sun, air, and water, and it grew a lot. It grew the second year but not as much as the first year. The third and fourth years, the tree grew about the same as the second year. The fifth year, the tree grew about the same as the first year. The sixth year, the tree either had a disease or did not get enough sun or water.

I planted this tree in 2000. For the first year, I watered it a lot and took care of it. It was a very pretty tree and grew a lot in the first year. The second, third, and fourth years, I got really bored with it and stopped watering it. It didn't grow much those years. Maybe it grew a couple of inches but that's all. In 2004, I decided that my tree was very special, and I started to water it more. It really grew that year. But the next year, I got too busy to water it very much, and it grew very little.

2. a.

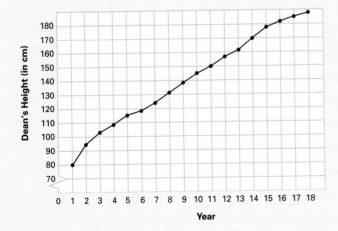

Hints and Comments

Materials

Student Activity Sheet 4 (one per student); compass (one per student); centimeter rulers (one per student)

Overview

Students use the Check Your Work problems as self-assessment. The answers to these problems are provided in the Student Book.

b. Discuss your answer with a classmate. Sample answer:
- From Dean's second birthday until his sixteenth birthday, he grew very regularly.
- After his sixteenth birthday, Dean's growth started to slow down, but he may still get taller after his nineteenth birthday.

c. According to the graph, Dean had his biggest growth spurt between his first and second birthdays. Dean grew 15 cm that year. But his length at birth is missing from the graph, so maybe he had his biggest growth spurt during his first year.

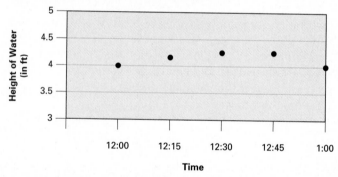

A Trendy Graphs

Mr. Akimo owns a tree nursery. He measures the circumference of the tree trunks to check their growth. One spring, he selected two trees of different species to study. Both had trunks that measured 2 inches in circumference. For the next two springs, he measured the circumference of both tree trunks. The results are shown in the table.

	Circumference (in inches)		
	First Measurement	Second Measurement	Third Measurement
Tree 1	2.0	3.0	4.9
Tree 2	2.0	5.5	7.1

3. a. Which tree will most likely have the larger circumference when Mr. Akimo measures them again next spring? Explain how you got your answer.

b. **Reflect** Do you get better information about the growth of the circumference of these trees by looking at the tables or by looking at the graphs? Explain your answer.

For Further Reflection
The reflection question is meant to summarize and extend what students have learned in the section.

◣ **For Further Reflection**

This graph indicates the height of water in a swimming pool from 12:00 noon to 1:00 P.M. Write a story that describes why the water levels change and at what times. Be specific.

Assessment Pyramid

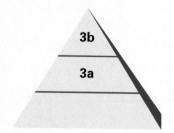

3b

3a

Assesses Section A Goals

Reaching All Learners

Writing Opportunity

Problem 3b would be a good problem to have students write about the advantages and disadvantages of the different representations: the table, graph, and growth story (which can be told in words or shown in a cross section drawing).

Solutions and Samples

3. a. The first tree will have the larger circumference. You may give an explanation by looking at the table, or you may make a graph and reason about the trend this graph shows.

Sample responses:

- Looking for patterns in the table:
The first tree is growing by an increasing amount every year, while the second tree is growing by a decreasing amount every year. You can see this in the tables using arrows with numbers that represent the differences.

Circumference (in inches)		
First Measurement	**Second Measurement**	**Third Measurement**
Tree 1 2.0	3.0	4.9

+1.0 in   +1.9 in

Circumference (in inches)		
First Measurement	**Second Measurement**	**Third Measurement**
Tree 2 2.0	5.5	7.1

+3.5 in   +1.6 in

- The first tree might grow as much as 4 in, putting it at 8.9 in. The second tree will probably grow less than 1 in, putting it at about 8 in. Make two graphs and reason about the trend the graphs show.

b. You may prefer either the graph or the table. You might prefer the table because it has the actual numbers, and you can calculate the exact change each year and use those numbers to make a decision. You might prefer the graph because you can see the trend in the growth of each tree and also the relationship between the two trees.

Growth of Trees 1 and 2

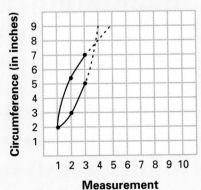

Hints and Comments

Overview

Students use the Check Your Work problems as self-assessment. The answers to these problems are provided in the Student Book.

Comments About the Solutions

For problem 3, it is important that students realize that although they can find a growth pattern, it is not certain that the same pattern will continue.

For Further Reflection

Answers will vary. Sample solution: On most days the local pool opens for swim practice from noon until 1 P.M. One group shows up at noon and practices for 45 minutes. Another group shows up at around 12:15 and practices for about 40 minutes. As more swimmers get in the pool the water level rises. When everyone leaves the pool at 1 P.M., the water level drops back down to 4 feet.

Section Focus

The situations studied in this section all involve equal increase over equal time periods or a constant rate of growth. This plays an important role in making formulas to represent these situations. For students, it is not obvious that all situations investigated in this section can be described by the same mathematical concept of linear growth.

It is the focus of this section to recognize and use linear growth by looking at the differences in a table; looking at the graph, which is a straight line; or looking at the formula that describes the situation. Both recursive (NEXT-CURRENT) and direct formulas are used.

Pacing and Planning

Day 4: The Marathon		Student pages 13–16
INTRODUCTION	Problem 1	Discuss the physiology of keeping cool while running a marathon.
CLASSWORK	Problems 2–5	Create and interpret a graph of the body temperature of a marathon runner.
HOMEWORK	Problems 6–9	Graph the linear growth of the radius of a tree.

Day 5: What's Next? (Continued)		Student pages 16–18
INTRODUCTION	Review homework.	Review homework from Day 4.
CLASSWORK	Problems 10–17	Write NEXT-CURRENT and direct formulas to represent linear growth of hair.
HOMEWORK	Problems 18–20	Graph and write a direct formula to represent linear growth of fingernails.

Day 6: Renting a Motorcycle		Student pages 18–22
INTRODUCTION	Review homework.	Review homework from Day 5.
CLASSWORK	Problems 21–26	Graph and write a direct formula to compare the different rates for renting motorcycles.
HOMEWORK	Check Your Work	Student self-assessment: Write recursive and direct formulas for linear growth patterns.

Day 7: Mid-unit assessment		
INTRODUCTION	Review homework.	Review homework from Day 6.
REVIEW	Sections A–B review	Review Summary pages from Sections A and B.
ASSESSMENT	Quiz #1	Assesses Section A and B Goals

Additional Resources: *Algebra Tools*; Additional Practice, Section B, pages 49 and 50

Materials

Student Resources

Quantities listed are per student.

- **Student Activity Sheets 5 and 6**

Teachers Resources

No resources required.

Student Materials

Quantities listed are per pair of students.

- Calculator
- Graph paper (one sheet per student)
- Colored pencils, one box

* See Hints and Comments for optional materials.

Learning Lines

Linear Relationships

Students investigate linear growth in a variety of situations. They identify whether or not the growth is linear and use tables, graphs, and formulas to describe linear growth. Direct formulas, such as $L = 2 + 1.5 \times T$, are used and interpreted. The first differences in a table of values for a linear formula are equal for equal periods of time.

Time (in months)	0	1	2	3	4
Length of Hair (in cm)	2	3.5	5	6.5	8

first differences   + 1.5   + 1.5   + 1.5

Students solve problems by comparing graphs and formulas involving linear relationships within the context of comparing two motorcycle rental companies. They informally identify steepness of the graph as represented by the price per mile and the *y*-intercept as the fixed starting amount. The point of intercept is only introduced informally by comparing graphs that represent both companies' formulas for calculating rental prices.

At the End of the Section: Learning Outcomes

Students write and use recursive and direct formulas to represent linear growth patterns. They solve problems by comparing different linear growth patterns. They know how to recognize linear growth within a variety of contexts by considering differences in a table or by considering the shape of a graph.

You might begin this section by reading and discussing the text and completing problem 1 as a whole-class activity.

You might ask students how far 40 km is (about 25 mi) and how long it might take someone to run it. (If someone ran at an average speed of 10 km per hour, it would take him or her 4 hours to run this distance.)

You may also briefly discuss how a person's body temperature rises as a result of strenuous exercise, such as running.

B Linear Patterns

The Marathon

In 490 B.C., there was a battle between the Greeks and the Persians near the village of Marathon. Legend tells us that immediately after the Greeks won, a Greek soldier was sent from Marathon to Athens to tell the city the good news. He ran the entire 40 kilometers (km). When he arrived, he was barely able to stammer out the news before he died.

1. What might have caused the soldier's death?

Marathon runners need lots of energy to run long distances. Your body gets energy to run by burning food. Just like in the engine of a car, burning fuel generates heat. Your body must release some of this heat or it will be seriously injured.

Reaching All Learners

Extension

Have students research the history of the marathon in more detail than the story on this page. They could investigate why the marathon is now 42.195 km, and not the original 40 km. Students could also look up times for the most recent Olympic marathon to get a better sense of world-class times for this popular event.

Solutions and Samples

1. Answers will vary. Some students may say that the soldier died from heat exhaustion, lack of water or food, or a heart attack.

Hints and Comments

Overview

Students read and discuss the history of the marathon run.

Comments About the Solutions

1. The purpose of this introductory question is to get students thinking about the fact that the body gets its energy from burning food calories and that heat is one of the by-products of converting food into energy.

Interdisciplinary Connection

You might ask science or health teachers in your grade level to teach a unit on nutrition, emphasizing the impact that food and exercise have on a person's metabolism and energy level.

Naoko Takahashi won the women's marathon during the 2000 Olympics. She finished the race in 2 hours, 23 minutes, and 14 seconds. She was the first Japanese woman to win an Olympic gold medal in track and field. Today the marathon is 42.195 km long, not the original 40.

2a It is not necessary that students make a table for the whole period of the marathon. A table that goes up to 30 minutes will suffice.

2b Make sure that every student's graph is a straight line. If students have difficulty determining where to plot the first point on the graph, you may tell them that the normal body temperature is about 98.6°F (37°C).

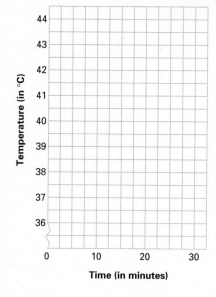

Normal body temperature for humans is 37° Centigrade (C), or 98.6° Fahrenheit (F). At a temperature of 41°C (105.8°F), the body's cells stop growing. At temperatures above 42°C (107.6°F), the brain, kidneys, and other organs suffer permanent damage.

When you run a marathon, your body produces enough heat to cause an increase in body temperature of 0.17°C every minute.

2. a. Make a table showing how your body temperature would rise while running a marathon if you did nothing to cool off. Show temperatures every 10 minutes.

   b. Use the table to make a graph of this data on **Student Activity Sheet 5**.

3. a. Why is the graph for problem 2b not realistic?

   b. What does your body do to compensate for the rising temperature?

Reaching All Learners

Intervention

You may need to review common strategies for multiplying by 10. Expand to multiplying by 100, 1000, etc. Remind students that multiplying by 20 is the same as multiplying by 10 and doubling the answer.

Solutions and Samples

2. a.

Time (in minutes)	10	20	30	40
Rise in Body Temperature (in °C)	1.7	3.4	5.1	6.8

or

Time (in minutes)	0	10	20	30	40
Body Temperature (in °C)	37	38.7	40.4	42.1	43.8

b.

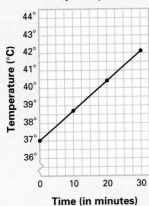

Body Temperature

3. a. Answers will vary. Sample response:

The line graph shows a body temperature of 42°C after 30 minutes of running, which is too high a temperature for the body to function well.

b. Your body sweats, which helps to lower the body temperature.

Materials

Student Activity Sheet 5 (one per student)

Overview

Students make a table and a graph that show a marathon runner's body temperature over time if his or her temperature keeps rising by 0.17°C per minute.

About the Mathematics

In Section A, students learned about patterns of increase and decrease by looking at the differences in the growth of one thing over equal time periods. In this section, linear patterns, situations that have equal increases over equal time periods, are investigated. The graphs for these situations are all straight lines. The fact that there are equal increases, or a constant rate of growth, plays an important role in making formulas for these situations.

Planning

Students may work on problems 2 and 3 in pairs or in small groups. You may wish to discuss problems 2 and 3 before students continue with problems 4 and 5 on the next page.

B Linear Patterns

Notes

5 Remind students how long it took Takahashi to run the marathon from the top of the previous page. (2 hr 23 min.)

Have students point out what they need to do with the time to solve this problem (convert to minutes).

When the body temperatures of marathon runners rise by about 1°C, their bodies begin to sweat to prevent the temperature from rising further. Then the body temperature neither increases nor decreases.

4. Use this information to redraw the line graph from problem 2b on **Student Activity Sheet 5**.

During the race, the body will lose about $\frac{1}{5}$ of a liter of water every 10 minutes.

5. How much water do you think Naoko Takahashi lost during the women's marathon in the 2000 Olympics?

What's Next?

Here you see a core sample of a tree. When this sample was taken, the tree was six years old.

6. What can you tell about the growth of the tree?

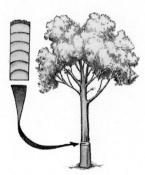

The table shows the radius for each year. Remember that the radius of a circle—in this problem, a growth ring—is half the diameter.

Year	1	2	3	4	5	6
Radius (in mm)	4	8	12	16	20	24

+4 +4 +4 +4 +4

7. Use the table to draw a graph.

7 Make sure that students connect the plotted points to make one continuous (straight) line. This is acceptable because growth is a continuous process.

Assessment Pyramid

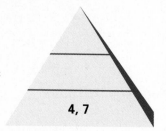

4, 7

Use information about increase and decrease to create line graphs.

Reaching All Learners

Intervention

If students have difficulty starting this problem, you might suggest that they make a ratio table showing the amount of time in minutes and the amount of water lost in liters. Students can then use the ratio table to determine the total water Naoko Takahashi lost during the race.

Solutions and Samples

4.

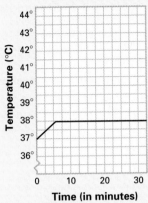

Body Temperature

5. Accept answers in the range of 2.8−3.0 liters of water. Sample strategy using a ratio table:

× 14

Time (in minutes)	10	140
Water (in liters)	$\frac{1}{5}$	$\frac{14}{5} = 2\frac{4}{5}$

6. The growth is very regular. The rings are all the same distance apart in the drawing, 4 mm.

7.

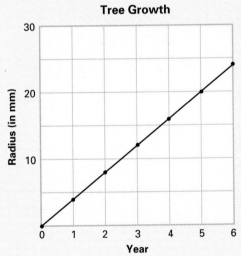

Tree Growth

Note: If the differences in the second row of the table are equal, the growth is linear. Of course this is the case only if the years in the first row are successive or show constant differences as well.

Hints and Comments

Materials

Student Activity Sheet 5, one per student (the same sheet used for problem 2b).

Overview

Students continue investigating the graph of a runner's body temperature over time. They redraw the graph taking into account one way the body cools itself. Then they start to investigate linear growth by examining a core sample of a tree that shows rings with equal thickness.

Comments About the Solutions

5. Because the human body does not begin to sweat until the body temperature rises 1°C, which will take about 6 minutes in this situation, students need to subtract 6 minutes from the total running time to determine the amount of water lost during the race.

Notes

8 This problem sets the stage for problem 9. Although students can easily find the answer for part **a** by extending the given table, this strategy is rather time-consuming for part **b**. This is intended to motivate a more efficient method.

9 This is the first problem in which students are asked to express a pattern using a formula.

Briefly discuss students' solutions and strategies, focusing on problems with which they had difficulty.

The graph you made is a straight line. Whenever a graph is a straight line, the growth is called linear growth. (In this case, the tree grew linearly.) In the table, you can see the growth is linear because the differences in the second row are equal. The change from one year to the next was the same for all of the years.

8. a. What might have been the size of the radius in year 7? Explain how you found your answer.

   b. Suppose the tree kept growing in this way. One year the radius would be 44 millimeters (mm). What would the radius be one year later?

If you know the radius of the tree in a certain year, you can always find the radius of the tree in the year that follows if it keeps growing linearly. In other words, if you know the radius of the CURRENT year, you can find the radius of the NEXT year.

9. If this tree continues growing linearly, how can you find the radius of the NEXT year from the radius of any CURRENT year? Write a formula.

The formula you wrote in problem 9 is called a **NEXT-CURRENT formula**.

Here you see the cross sections of two more trees. You could make graphs showing the yearly radius for each of these trees, too.

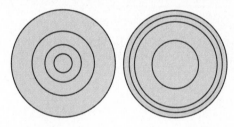

10. a. Will the graphs be straight lines or not? How can you tell without drawing the graphs?

   b. Describe the shape of the graph for each tree. You may want to make a graph first.

Reaching All Learners

Intervention

If students have difficulty seeing the relationship in problem 9, you may need to continue to ask students to extend the pattern additional years.

Vocabulary Building

Some students might be familiar with this term, NEXT-CURRENT, from earlier algebra units, such as *Building Formulas*. If so, have these students explain or give an example of this type of formula. A NEXT-CURRENT formula is also called a recursive formula.

Solutions and Samples

8. a. 28 mm. The radius increases by 4 mm each year. The radius of the tree was 24 mm during year 6. So 24 + 4 = 28 mm.

b. 48 mm

9. If you add 4 to the radius of the CURRENT year, you can find the radius of NEXT year.

A formula for the radius of the tree in succeeding years is:

NEXT = CURRENT + 4, or

CURRENT + 4 = NEXT

Note: A NEXT-CURRENT formula is also known as a *recursive formula*.

10. a. No. Sample explanation:

The rings are not equally spaced, so neither radius is growing steadily (increasing at the same rate).

b. Sample description:
First tree: the graph will become steeper and steeper because the radius is growing faster and faster.

Second tree: the graph will become less steep and level off because the radius grows quickly during the first two years, and then it slows down and grows at a constant rate.

Hints and Comments

Overview

Students investigate linear growth by examining a core sample of a tree that shows rings with equal thickness.

About the Mathematics

On this page, students are using recursive formulas such as NEXT = CURRENT + 4. These formulas were introduced in the unit *Building Formulas*. The relationship between CURRENT and NEXT can be found by investigating the pattern in the rows of a table as shown below.

Year	1	2	3	4
Radius (in mm)	4	8	12	16

+ 4   + 4   + 4

This relationship can also be expressed as a word formula. You can find the size of the radius for NEXT year by adding 4 mm to the radius for the CURRENT year. An arrow string can also be used:

$$\text{CURRENT} \xrightarrow{\ +\,4\,mm\ } \text{NEXT}$$

Planning

Students may work on problems 8–10 in any setting. These problems may also be assigned as homework.

Comments About the Solutions

8. At this point, some students may see a need for a more efficient method to find a solution, such as the recursive NEXT-CURRENT formula, made explicit after problem 9.

B Linear Patterns

Notes

13 Encourage students to show or explain how they got their answers. Students who have answers of 22 or 26 cm may have mistakenly used the given table as a ratio table.

16a Students should see that due to order of operations, the expression $2 + 1.5T$ is the same as $1.5T + 2$. Multiplication is done before addition.

16b You may want to explain to students that this is called a *direct formula* because you can calculate the length of hair at any time without needing to add 1.5 for each month.

Hair and Nails

Paul went to get a haircut. When he got home, he looked in the mirror and screamed, "It's too short!"

He decided not to get his hair cut again for a long time. In the meantime, he decided to measure how fast his hair grew. Below is a table that shows the length of Paul's hair (in centimeters) as he measured it each month.

Time (in months)	0	1	2	3	4	5	6
Length (in cm)	2	3.5	5	6.5			

11. How long was Paul's hair after the haircut?

12. a. How long will his hair be in five months?

  b. Why is it easy to calculate this length?

13. a. How long will Paul's hair be after a year if it keeps growing at the same rate and he does not get a haircut?

  b. Draw a graph showing how Paul's hair grows over a year if he does not get a haircut.

  c. Describe the shape of this graph.

14. If Paul's hair is 10 cm long at some point, how long will it be one month later?

If you know the length of Paul's hair in the current month, you can use it to find his hair length for the next month.

15. Write a formula using *NEXT* and *CURRENT*.

You knew that the beginning length of Paul's hair was 2 cm. That's why it is possible to make a **direct formula** for Paul's hair growth:

$$L = 2 + 1.5T$$

16. a. What do you think the letter L stands for? The letter T?

  b. Explain the numbers in the formula.

Assessment Pyramid

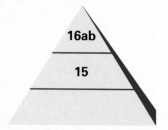

Use algebraic models to represent realistic situations.

Describe linear growth with recursive formulas.

Reaching All Learners

Intervention

If students have difficulty writing the NEXT-CURRENT formula in problem 15, point out the information gained from problem 14. You might also help students to write a word formula first. Ask, *How can you find Paul's hair length for the next month?* (You can find the length of his hair the next month by adding 1.5 cm to the current length.) You could also suggest that students express the growth pattern using an arrow string.

Vocabulary Building

A direct formula can be used to find a value for any given number. To use a NEXT-CURRENT formula, the starting number (or previous number) must be known.

Solutions and Samples

11. 2 cm

12. a. 9.5 cm

   b. Sample explanation:

     It is easy to calculate the new hair length because his hair grows the same amount (1.5 cm) every month.

13. a. 20 cm. Sample strategies:

- Some students might extend the table and fill in lengths for the remaining six months.

Time (in months)	0	6	7	8	9	10	11	12
Length (in cm)	2	11	12.5	14	15.5	17	18.5	20

+ 3   + 3

- In 12 months, Paul's hair grew 18 cm (12 × 1.5 = 18 cm). His hair was originally 2 cm long, so after one year, his hair length will be 2 + 18 = 20 cm long.

   b.

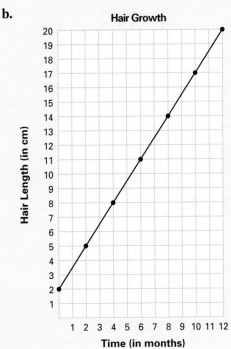

Hair Growth

   c. The graph of Paul's hair growth is a straight line.

14. 11.5 cm

15. NEXT = CURRENT + 1.5, or

   CURRENT + 1.5 = NEXT

16. a. *L* stands for length of the hair (cm); *T* stands for time in months.

   b. The number 2 is the length of Paul's hair after the haircut. The number 1.5 stands for the amount his hair (cm) grows each month. It grows 1.5 cm each month.

Hints and Comments

Materials

graph paper, one sheet per student

Overview

Students investigate a person's hair growth using the data in a table. They draw a graph and make predictions about what his hair length would be in five months. They write a NEXT-CURRENT formula to describe the hair growth and are introduced to a direct formula describing the same hair growth.

About the Mathematics

A table is a strong tool to investigate growth patterns. Students may now feel comfortable with the concept of growth rate. In the table, the growth rate is 1.5 cm per month. Because the differences in length for every two consecutive months are equal, this is a linear growth pattern. The graph is a straight line.

Planning

Students may work individually on problems 11–15. You may also assign these problems as homework. Discuss the notation used in the formula after students complete this problem.

Comments About the Solutions

11.–14.

   The purpose of these problems is to help students begin thinking about how to write a direct formula to represent this hair-growth situation.

13. Distinguish the table of values here from a ratio table. Relate the data in the table to the graph. Students should learn to recognize linearity from a table, a graph, and a formula.

16. The purpose of this problem is to help students realize the importance of knowing what the words and/or symbols used in a formula represent. By this point in the unit, most students should understand what each letter in the formula represents and how the formula originated. If students are having difficulty, you might suggest that they write a word formula to represent this pattern:

You can find the hair length for a given month by adding 1.5 cm to the previous month's hair length.

Students may write the direct formula in different orders:

$2 + 1.5 \times T = L$ or

$2 + T \times 1.5 = L$.

B Linear Patterns

Notes

17 Students may use two different growth rates in their formulas, 1.4 cm (the monthly rate) or 16.8 cm (the yearly rate). In the latter case, the T must represent the number of years rather than the number of months.

18 To prompt student thinking about solving this problem, you may ask, *If Sean's hair is 5 cm in January and 29 cm at the end of December, how much did it grow each month, on average?* (2 cm per month.)

18 After solving this problem you may want to ask, *Why do you divide 8 mm by 4 when there are only three empty rows in the table?* (Think: 4 months.)

Sacha's hair is 20 cm long and grows at a constant rate of 1.4 cm a month.

17. Write a direct formula with L and T to describe the growth of Sacha's hair.

Time (in months)	Fingernail Length (in mm)
0	15
1	
2	
3	
4	23

Suppose you decided not to cut one fingernail for several months, and the nail grew at a constant rate. The table shows the lengths of a nail in millimeters at the beginning and after four months.

18. How much did this nail grow every month?

19. Predict what the graph that fits the data in the table looks like. If you cannot predict its shape, think of some points you might use to draw the graph.

20. Write a direct formula for fingernail growth using L for length (in millimeters) and T for time (in months).

Renting a Motorcycle

During the summer months, many people visit Townsville. A popular tourist activity there is to rent a motorcycle and take a one-day tour through the mountains.

You can rent motorcycles at E.C. Rider Motorcycle Rental and at Budget Cycle Rental. The two companies calculate their rental prices in different ways.

The most popular trip this season goes from Townsville, through Cove Creek, to Overlook Point, and back through Meadowville.

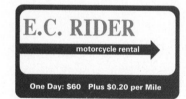

One Day: $60   Plus $0.20 per Mile

cycle rental
One Day: Just $0.75 per Mile

Assessment Pyramid

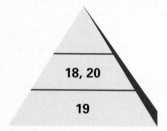

18, 20

19

Describe linear growth using direct formulas.

Use information about increase to create graphs.

Reaching All Learners

Intervention

If students are having difficulty with the fingernail problems, suggest that they determine how many millimeters the fingernail grew between the first month and fourth month (8 mm) and remind them that the fingernail is growing at a constant rate.

Advanced Learners

Problem: Sonya's hair grew 14.4 cm in one year. Make a graph that shows the length of Sonya's hair over one year if she goes to the hairdresser every two months. Explain the assumptions you made.

Solutions and Samples

17. $L = 20 + 1.4T$

18. 2 mm. Strategies will vary. Some students might reason that a growth pattern of 8 mm over a four-month period is the same as 2 mm per month.

19. The graph will be a straight line because the length of the nail grows the same amount each month.

20. $L = 15 + 2T$

Hints and Comments

Overview

Students explain a direct formula that describes hair growth. They write this type of formula to describe the hair growth of another person. Then they investigate the linear growth pattern of fingernails. They write a formula, use a table, and predict what the graph will look like for this growth pattern.

About the Mathematics

The relationship between the various representations of a linear relationship, table, direct formula, and graph, is emphasized. Formulas like $L = 2 + 1.5 \times T$ are called *direct formulas*. All linear growth situations can be described with a direct formula similar to this one. Formulas and linear equations are studied more extensively in the unit *Graphing Equations*.

The remaining problems in this section will reinforce students' understanding of linear growth patterns and formulas. These problems will also provide students with enough experiences to begin to understand the concepts of *intercept* and *slope*, which are made explicit in the unit *Graphing Equations*.

These problems involve linear growth patterns. Students should see the similarities between these situations and the situations of hair and nail growth. They all deal with equal increases over equal time periods. The hair growth situation may be used as a model to show students an example of linear increase.

B Linear Patterns

Notes

Encourage students to discuss their solutions together, in pairs or small groups, before they begin each new problem.

21 Students must realize that they can use the distance mentioned in the introduction to the problem to calculate the price that each company charges.

23c Be sure that students use different colored pencils to indicate different graphs and write the formula's name next to each graph.

24a Students should be able to write the 0.20*M* part of the formula. Make sure students use the right formulas to draw their graphs.

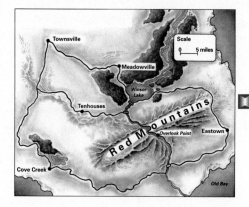

Even though more and more people are making this 170-mile trip, the owner of Budget Cycle Rental noticed that her business is getting worse. This is very surprising to her, because her motorcycles are of very good quality.

21. Reflect What do you think explains the decrease in Budget's business compared to E.C. Rider's?

The rental price you pay depends on the number of miles you ride. With Budget Cycle Rental, the price goes up $0.75 for every mile you ride.

22. a. How much does the cost go up per mile with a rental from E.C. Rider?

 b. Does that mean it is always less expensive to rent from E.C. Rider? Explain your answer.

Budget Cycle Rental uses this rental formula: $P = 0.75M$.

23. a. Explain each part of this formula.

 b. What formula does E.C. Rider use?

 c. Graph both formulas on **Student Activity Sheet 6**.

Ms. Rider is thinking about changing the rental price for her motorcycles. This will also change her formula. She thinks about raising the starting amount from $60 to $70.

24. a. What would the new formula be?

 b. Do you think Ms. Rider's idea is a good one? Why or why not?

Budget Cycle Rental is going to change prices too. See the new sign.

25. a. Write the new formula for Budget Cycle Rental.

 b. Make a graph of this new formula on **Student Activity Sheet 6**. You may want to make a table first.

26. Look again at the 170-mile trip from Townsville. Whom would you rent your motorcycle from now, given the new information from problems 24 and 25?

Assessment Pyramid

Recognize the power of graphs for solving problems.

Describe linear growth with direct formulas.

Reaching All Learners

Accommodation

For some students you may want to provide the outline for tables for E.C. Rider and Budget, either on the overhead or handouts, to support their construction of graphs for each formula. Most students will need to make tables before they will be able to draw a graph of both formulas.

Solutions and Samples

21. Most people rent where it is the least expensive.

E.C. Rider's charge for the trip would be

$60.00 + 170 \times \$0.20 = \$94.00$.

Budget's charge for the trip would be

$170 \times \$0.75 = \$127.50$.

It is less expensive to rent from E.C. Rider for this trip.

22. a. 20 cents per mile

b. No. Explanations will vary. Sample explanation:

The better choice depends on the length of the trip. To rent a motorcycle from E.C. Rider for a 10-mile trip would cost $60 + 10 \times \$0.20 = \$62.00$. To rent from Budget for the same distance would cost $10 \times \$0.75 = \$7.50$.

23. a. *P* represents the price or cost in dollars. *M* represents the number of miles of the trip. The price you pay per mile is $0.75.

b. $P = 60 + 0.20M$

c.

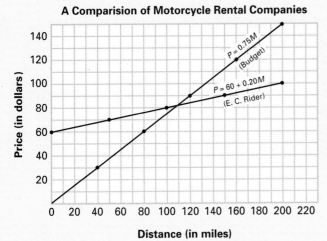

A Comparision of Motorcycle Rental Companies

P = 0.75M (Budget)
P = 60 + 0.20M (E. C. Rider)

24. a. $P = 70 + 0.20M$

b. Answers may vary. Sample response:

Ms. Rider's price will still be cheaper than Budget's price for the most popular trip, so I think it is a good idea.

Hints and Comments

Materials

Student Activity Sheet 6, one per student; colored pencils (one box per student)

Overview

Students compare motorcycle rental prices of two companies. They write formulas to represent the rental pricing structure of both companies. Then they draw a graph to compare the two companies' rental prices. They investigate the influence on the formula and graph if the situation changes.

About the Mathematics

E.C. Rider charges $0.20 per mile. This is the amount of growth per month. This number determines the *steepness* of the graph. E.C. Rider's charges start with an amount of $60. This is analogous to the beginning length in the hair-growth context. This number can be found where the graph starts on the vertical axis.

As students draw their graphs in problems 23 and 25, they might notice that the starting point for the new graph line for each company's rental formula is translated. Also, the points of intersection (that indicate trips for which the price is the same for either company) are different. The new graph lines still have the same steepness (slope).

Comments About the Solutions

22. b. Students may have already noticed that a short trip would be more expensive at E.C. Rider because of the company's fixed charge of $60.

25. a. $P = 0.75 (M - 20)$, or $(M - 20) \times 0.75 = P$

b.

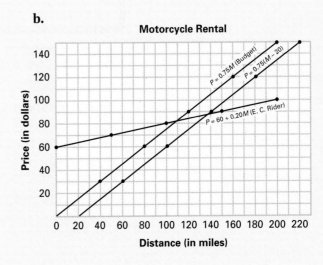

Motorcycle Rental

P = 0.75M (Budget)
P = 0.75(M - 20)
P = 60 + 0.20M (E. C. Rider)

26. E.C. Rider's price, $104, is cheaper than Budget's price, $112.50.

Notes

The Summary for this section reiterates each representation for linear functions addressed in this section. Be sure to go through the Summary carefully, having students read parts aloud. It is critical that students review the relationship between tables, graphs, and recursive and direct formulas presented in this section.

 Linear Patterns

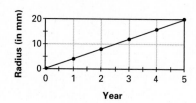 **Summary**

The situations in this section were all examples of graphs with straight lines. A graph with a straight line describes *linear growth*. The rate of change is constant. The differences over *equal time periods* will always be the same.

You can recognize linear growth by looking at the differences in a table or by considering the shape of the graph.

Year	1	2	3	4	5
Radius (in mm)	4	8	12	16	20

+4   +4   +4   +4

Core Sample of a Tree

Linear growth can be described using formulas. A *NEXT-CURRENT formula* that fits this table and graph is:

NEXT = CURRENT + 4

A *direct formula* that fits this table and graph is:

radius = year number × 4 or R = 4Y

with the radius measured in millimeters.

Reaching All Learners

Parent Involvement

Have students discuss the Summary and Check Your Work problems with their parents. The representations of linear patterns may be familiar to some parents. Parents may benefit from helping their child look for problems from Section B similar to the Check Your Work problems.

Writing Opportunity

Have students write in their own words how linear growth can be recognized from a formula, a table, and a graph.

Hints and Comments

Overview

Students summarize what they have learned about linear growth by making tables, formulas, and graphs of linear situations.

Notes

1 Note that this problem does not describe a continuous situation. Therefore the dots in a graph should not be connected. Even though students are not asked to draw the graph, you might want to discuss this point.

Check Your Work

1. Lucia earns $12 per week babysitting.

   a. Make a table to show how much money Lucia earns over six weeks.

   b. Write a formula using *NEXT* and *CURRENT* to describe Lucia's earnings.

   c. Write a direct formula using *W* (week) and *E* (earnings) to describe Lucia's earnings.

Time (in weeks)	0	1	2	3
Length (in cm)	11	12.4	13.8	15.2

2. **a.** Show that the growth described in the table is linear.

   b. Write a formula using *NEXT* and *CURRENT* for the example.

   c. Write a direct formula using *L* (length) and *T* (time) for the example.

   Sonya's hair grew about 14.4 cm in one year. It is possible to write the following formulas:

   $$NEXT = CURRENT + 14.4$$
   $$NEXT = CURRENT + 1.2$$

3. Explain what each formula represents.

Assessment Pyramid

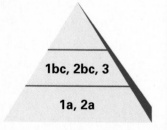

1bc, 2bc, 3

1a, 2a

Assesses Section B Goals

Reaching All Learners

Intervention

For problem 3, if students do not see the relationship between each formula, ask, *What is the relationship between the numbers, 14.4 and 1.2? What is the relationship between 144 and 12?*

Vocabulary Building

Have students write an explanation of the differences between NEXT-CURRENT (recursive) and direct formulas. Include the advantages and disadvantages of each.

Solutions and Samples

Answers to Check Your Work

1. a. table:

Time (in weeks)	0	1	2	3	4	5	6
Earnings (in dollars)	0	12	24	36	48	60	72

It is all right if you started your table with week 1.

b. recursive formula: NEXT = CURRENT + 12

c. direct formula: $E = 12W$, with E in dollars and W in weeks.

2. a. The table shows that the length grows each month by the same amount; the differences are all equal to 1.4 cm.

b. NEXT = CURRENT + 1.4

c. $L = 11 + 1.4T$, with L in centimeters and T in weeks.

3. The first formula gives Sonya's hair growth each year, so *NEXT* stands for next year, *CURRENT* stands for the current year, and 14.4 stands for the number of centimeters her hair grows yearly.

The second formula gives her hair growth each month, so *NEXT* stands for next month, *CURRENT* stands for the current month, and 1.2 stands for the number of centimeters her hair grows monthly.

Hints and Comments

Overview

Students use the Check Your Work problems as self-assessment. The answers to these problems are provided in the Student Book.

 Linear Patterns

Lamar has started his own company that provides help for people who have problems with their computer. On his website, he uses a sign that reads:

> **HELP needed for computer problems? We visit you at your home. You pay only $12.00 for the house call and $10.00 for each half hour of service!**

4. Write a direct formula that can be used by Lamar's company.

Suppose you want to start your own help desk for computer problems. You want to be less costly than Lamar, and you suppose that most jobs will not take over two hours.

5. a. Make your own sign for a website.

   b. Make a direct formula you can use. Show why your company is a better choice than Lamar's.

For Further Reflection

For Further Reflection

The reflection question is meant to summarize and extend what students have learned in the section.

Refer to the original prices for E.C. Rider Motorcycle Rentals and Budget Rental Cycles. Describe in detail a trip that would make it better to rent from Budget than from E.C. Rider.

One Day: $60 Plus $0.20 per Mile

cycle rental
One Day: Just $0.75 per Mile

Assessment Pyramid

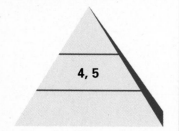

4, 5

Assesses Section B Goals

Reaching All Learners

Intervention

Students who have a difficult time finding a direct formula should be encouraged to find a NEXT-CURRENT formula first. For the babysitter, the recursive formula would be NEXT = CURRENT + 12. Then ask students if they can recall the relationship between the steps in a recursive formula and the value used in a direct formula. (It is the rate of change.)

Solutions and Samples

4. Discuss your formula with a classmate. Your formula may differ from the examples shown below; you may have chosen other letters or used words. Sample formulas:

   - $E = 12 + 10T$ with earnings E in dollars and time T in half hours.
   - $E = 12 + 20T$ with earnings E in dollars and time T in hours.
   - amount (in dollars) = 12 + 10 × time (30 minutes)

5. **a.** Show your sign to your classmates.

   b. Discuss your formula with a classmate or in class. There are different ways to make a formula that yields a less costly result than Lamar's. You will have to show why it is less costly and give your reasoning. Some examples:

   - Make both the charge for a house call and the amount per half hour lower than in Lamar's formula. You will always be cheaper. For instance: $E = 10 + 8T$ with earnings E in dollars and time T in half hours.

   - Keep the call charge equal, but make the amount per half hour lower than in Lamar's formula. You will always be cheaper. For instance: $E = 12 + 8T$ with earnings E in dollars and time T in half hours.

   - Make the call charge higher and the amount per half hour lower than in Lamar's formula. For instance: $E = 20 + 8T$ with earnings E in dollars and time T in half hours.

     Your company will be cheaper after more than four half hours, but you will earn more for short calls. Make a note on your website that most jobs take an average of two hours.

For Further Reflection

Answers will vary. Sample solution: E.C. Rider rents bikes for $60 a day and 20 cents a mile. Budget Cycle Rental rents bikes for just 75 cents a mile. There is a cool waterfall that is about 20 miles from the rental shops. If I wanted to bike to the waterfall and was a smart shopper, I would rent a bike from Budget because I would only have to pay 75 cents × 20 miles = $15 (each way), or $30 total. Renting a bike from E.C. Rider would cost more than $60! If I rented from Budget, I could even take a short side trip and still save money!

Hints and Comments

Overview

Students use the Check Your Work problems as self-assessment. The answers to these problems are provided in the Student Book.

Planning

After students finish Section B, you may want to assign some additional practice from the Additional Practice Section in the Student Book.

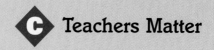

Section Focus

The surface area of a poplar leaf is used to investigate quadratic growth. Students investigate second differences in a table. They use quadratic formulas that describe quadratic growth within this context. The growth of aquatic weeds is used to introduce students to exponential growth.

Pacing and Planning

Day 8: Leaf Area		Student pages 23–27
INTRODUCTION	Problems 1–3	Write a direct formula for the area of a leaf.
CLASSWORK	Problems 4–6	Use tables and graphs to analyze the direct (quadratic) formula for the area of a leaf.
HOMEWORK	Problems 7–9	Graph the direct (quadratic) formula for the area of a leaf and use the graph and the formula to determine the area of leaves with various lengths.

Day 9: Water Lily		Student pages 27–28
INTRODUCTION	Review homework.	Review homework from Day 8.
CLASSWORK	Problems 10–13	Investigate the growth pattern of the radius of a circular leaf.
HOMEWORK	Problem 14	Extend and identify linear and quadratic growth patterns.

Day 10: Aquatic Weeds		Student pages 29–31
INTRODUCTION	Problem 15	Determine whether the growth in the area of a fast-growing aquatic weed is linear.
CLASSWORK	Problems 16–20	Use tables and graphs to investigate the growth of quantities that repeatedly double over time.
HOMEWORK	Problems 21 and 22	Use the concept of growth to predict the number of bacteria.

Day 11: Double Trouble (Continued)		Student pages 31–34
INTRODUCTION	Review homework.	Review homework from Day 10.
CLASSWORK	Problems 23–25	Investigate exponential growth.
HOMEWORK	Check Your Work	Student self-assessment: Graph, identify, and interpret growth patterns.

Additional Resources: *Algebra Tools*; Additional Practice, Section C, page 50

Materials

Student Resources

Quantities listed are per student.

● **Student Activity Sheets 7–11**

Teachers Resources

No resources required.

Student Materials

Quantities listed are per pair of students, unless otherwise noted.

● Calculator
● Centimeter ruler
● Colored pencils, one box
● Graph paper (two sheets per student)

* See Hints and Comments for optional materials.

Learning lines

Quadratic Relationships

If the "first differences" are not equal but the "second differences" are, the growth is *quadratic*. The table shows the relationship between length and area of squares. If the length increases by one centimeter each time, the first differences are not equal, but the second differences are equal.

Length of Square (in cm)	1	2	3	4	5	6
Surface Area of Square (in cm²)	1	4	9	16	25	36

first differences   +3 +5 +7 +9 +11

second differences   +2 +2 +2 +2

At this stage, students are not expected to construct quadratic formulas, but they use and adapt them. The formal term *parabola*, for the graph of a quadratic relationship, is not used.

Relationships Showing Exponential Growth

Students are introduced to situations involving exponential growth. In the table, this becomes visible if, at equal time periods, each entry in the table is found by multiplying by a growth factor. If each value in the table is found by multiplying by a *growth factor*, the growth is *exponential*. The table below shows the area covered by some weed that yearly grows by a growth factor of two. Notice that having a growth factor of two means that the area covered by the weed is doubling every year.

Year	1	2	3	4	5
Area Covered (in km²)	400	800	1,600	3,200	6,400

× 2   × 2   × 2   × 2

Only NEXT-CURRENT formulas are used to describe exponential growth.

At the End of This Section: Learning Outcomes

Students are able to discern whether growth as presented in a situation using tables is linear, quadratic, exponential, or none of these. They use and understand direct formulas for quadratic growth and recursive formulas for exponential growth.

Photosynthesis is discussed
here as a context to motivate
the need to find the surface
area of leaves.

1a Discuss in class what
surface area of a leaf
means. Some students
may mention you need
the area of both sides of
the leaf.

1b Remind students of
what they did in the unit
Reallotment, when they
compared the surface areas
of leaves by drawing their
outlines on grid paper.

C Differences in Growth

Leaf Area

The main function of leaves is to create food for the
entire plant. Each leaf absorbs light energy and uses it
to decompose the water in the leaf into its elements—
hydrogen and oxygen. The oxygen is released into the
atmosphere. The hydrogen is combined with carbon
dioxide from the atmosphere to create sugars that feed
the plant. This process is called *photosynthesis.*

1. **a.** Why do you think a leaf's ability to manufacture
   plant food might depend on its surface area?

   b. Describe a way to find the surface area of any of
   the leaves shown on the left.

The picture below shows three poplar leaves. Marsha states, "These
leaves are similar. Each leaf is a reduction of the previous one."

2. Measure the height and width of each of the leaves to determine
   whether Marsha is right.

Reaching All Learners

Hands On Learning

A direct connection to the measurement unit *Reallotment* can be made
before beginning this section. Bring in a small bag of leaves of various sizes.
Pass the bag around and have each student choose a leaf from the bag.
In pairs, have students share strategies for finding the area of the leaf they
selected. Some students might suggest tracing the outline of the leaf on
graph paper and counting the squares. Other students might suggest
measurement techniques that require rulers.

Solutions and Samples

1. a. Sample response:

A leaf with a larger surface area can absorb more light energy and carbon dioxide and holds more water within it, all of which are required in the manufacture of food.

b. Answers will vary. Students may suggest tracing a leaf onto a piece of graph paper and counting the squares within the shape, combining any partial squares.

2. Yes, Marsha is right, the leaves are similar; they have the same shape even though they are different sizes. The ratios of the length to width are the same in all figures.

Hints and Comments

Overview

Students explore different leaves and describe how to find their surface areas.

About the Mathematics

In the unit *Reallotment,* several strategies were used to determine the surface area of a leaf. Known mathematical shapes can quite easily model the leaf of a black poplar, which is why this leaf is used. *Similar* means having the same shape, the same ratio between the dimensions, and the same angles, but the dimensions (the measurements) themselves can be different. Similarity is also studied in the unit *It's All the Same.*

Interdisciplinary Connection

In science class, students may investigate in more depth how photosynthesis works.

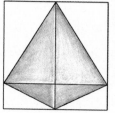

height

One way to estimate the surface area of a poplar leaf is to draw a square around it as shown in the diagram on the right.

The kite-shaped model on the left covers about the same portion of the square as the actual leaf on the left.

3a Students should understand that the square can be divided into four pieces so that half of each piece is shaded.

3. a. Approximately what portion of the square does the leaf cover? Explain your reasoning.

   b. If you know the height (*h*) of such a leaf, write a direct formula that you can use to calculate its area (*A*).

   c. If *h* is measured in centimeters, what units should be used to express *A*?

3d Emphasize that students need to draw only the outline of the leaf.

   d. The formula that you created in part **b** finds the area of poplar leaves that are symmetrical. Draw a picture of a leaf that is not symmetrical for which the formula will still work.

Area Differences

You can use this formula for the area of a poplar leaf when the height (*h*) is known:

$$A = \tfrac{1}{2} h^2$$

You can rewrite the formula using arrow language:

$$h \xrightarrow{\text{squared}} \cdots \xrightarrow{\times \frac{1}{2}} A$$

The table shows the areas of two poplar leaves.

Height (in cm)	6	7	8	9	10	11	12
Area (in cm²)	18	24.5					

   4. a. Verify that the areas for heights of 6 cm and 7 cm are correct in the table.

   b. On **Student Activity Sheet 7**, fill in the remaining area values in the table. Describe any patterns that you see.

   c. **Reflect** How do you know that the relationship between area and height is not linear?

Assessment Pyramid

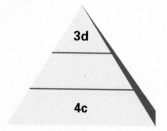

3d

4c

Use algebraic models to describe realistic situations.

Identify linear patterns in tables and graphs.

Reaching All Learners

Vocabulary Building

A *kite* is a shape defined in high school geometry. A quadrilateral is called a kite if one diagonal is both perpendicular to the other diagonal and cuts it in half (i.e., one diagonal is a perpendicular bisector of the other).

Intervention

You may want to have an enlarged overhead of the kite available to demonstrate the relationship between height and surface area. Have a student volunteer to demonstrate how they can "reallot" the model kite to form a rectangle that is half the area of the surrounding square.

Solutions and Samples

3. a. The leaf covers about half of the square. Sample explanations:

- In the kite-shaped model, if you fold the white part of the figure onto the shaded part, you will have completely covered the shaded part.

- The square can be divided into four smaller rectangles. About half of each rectangle is shaded, and half is white.

b. Formulas may vary. Sample formula:

$$A = \tfrac{1}{2} h^2$$

If the length of the side of the square is h, then the area of that square is h^2. Because the leaf has an area that is half of the area of the square, the formula for the area of the leaf is $A = \tfrac{1}{2} h^2$.

c. If the height is measured in centimeters, the area should be expressed in square centimeters.

d. Drawings will vary. Sample drawing:

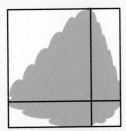

The center of the leaf in this example is shifted to the right.

4. a. $\tfrac{1}{2} \times 6^2 = \tfrac{1}{2} \times 36 = 18 \text{ cm}^2$

$\tfrac{1}{2} \times 7^2 = \tfrac{1}{2} \times 49 = 24.5 \text{ cm}^2$

b.

Height (in cm)	6	7	8	9	10	11	12
Area (in cm²)	18	24.5	32	40.5	50	60.5	72

Students may note the following patterns:

- For odd heights, the areas end with five-tenths.

- Each area is an increase over the previous area, first by 6.5, then by 7.5, then 8.5, then 9.5, and so on.

c. The relationship is not linear because for the same change in height, the changes in area are different. The differences in the second row of the table are not equal as shown in the answer for problem **b.**

Hints and Comments

Materials

graph paper (one sheet per student);
Student Activity Sheet 7 (one per student)

Overview

Students investigate the surface area of a black poplar leaf and create a direct formula for finding the area based on the height of the leaf. They draw a nonsymmetric leaf that can also be represented by the formula. They then use the formula to make a table for the areas of different black poplar leaves and investigate patterns in the table.

About the Mathematics

The area can be found by "reallotting" it, by cutting and pasting the original shape. Another strategy is to divide the given shape into smaller parts of which it is easy to determine the area. The formula for the area of a square is *length times length* or *length²*. Students should know this formula and the notation as well as an abbreviated form. Squares and square roots were introduced in the unit *Facts and Factors*.

Planning

You may wish to work through problem 3 as a whole class activity. Make sure students know how to work with the formula before they start working on problem 4.

Comments About the Solutions

4. b. Two patterns are apparent just by looking at the numbers in the table. The numbers increase and they are all halves of square numbers.

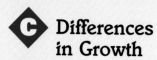
Differences in Growth

Notes

Before students begin the problems on this page, you may need to spend some time talking about the idea of differences.

The diagram below shows the differences between the areas of the first three leaves in the table.

Height (in cm)	6	7	8	9	10	11	12
Area (in cm²)	18	24.5	32	...?...	...?...	...?...	...?...

First Difference   6.5   7.5   ...?...   ...?...   ...?...   ...?...

5. a. On **Student Activity Sheet 7**, fill in the remaining "first difference" values. Do you see any patterns in the differences?

b. The first "first difference" value (6.5) is plotted on the graph on **Student Activity Sheet 8**. Plot the rest of the differences that you found in part **a** on this graph.

c. Describe your graph.

Height (in cm)	6	7	8	9	10	11	12
Area (in cm²)	18	24.5	32	...?...	...?...	...?...	...?...

First Difference   6.5   7.5   ...?...   ...?...   ...?...   ...?...

Second Difference   1   1   ...?...   ...?...   ...?...

As shown in the diagram, you can find one more row of differences, called the **second differences**.

6. a. Finish filling in the row of second differences in the diagram on **Student Activity Sheet 7**.

b. What do you notice about the second differences? If the diagram were continued to the right, find the next two second differences.

c. How can you use the patterns of the second differences and first differences to find the areas of leaves that have heights of 13 cm and 14 cm? Continue the diagram on **Student Activity Sheet 7** for these new values.

d. Use the area formula for poplar leaves ($A = \frac{1}{2}h^2$) to verify your work in part **c**.

Assessment Pyramid

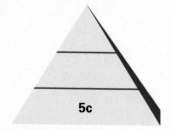

5c

Identify linear patterns in tables and graphs.

Reaching All Learners

Advanced Learners

For students who finish this page early, encourage them to make their own quadratic patterns. Have them start from the second differences and work backwards to build first differences and the original pattern. They should discover that they will need to address the question, *What do you need to know to use second differences to build first differences and the original pattern?* (You need to decide on a starting or ending, value.)

Solutions and Samples

5. a.

Height (in cm)	6	7	8	9	10	11	12
Area (in cm²)	18	24.5	32	40.5	50	60.5	72

6.5 7.5 8.5 9.5 10.5 11.5

The differences increase by one each time.

b.

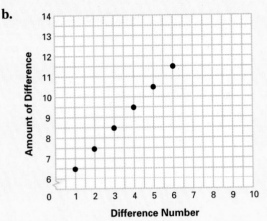

Difference Number

c. The points lie on a straight line.

6. a. See the diagram for part **c** below.

b. The second difference is always 1.

c. You begin with the 1 in the bottom row and work upward.

Height (in cm)	6	7	8	9	10	11	12	13	14
Area (in cm²)	18	24.5	32	40.5	50	60.5	72	84.5	98

First Difference 6.5 7.5 8.5 9.5 10.5 11.5 12.5 13.5

Second Difference 1 1 1 1 1 1 1

d. $A = \frac{1}{2} \times 13^2 = 84.5$ cm²;

$A = \frac{1}{2} \times 14^2 = 98$ cm².

Hints and Comments

Materials

Student Activity Sheet 7, (one per student);
Student Activity Sheet 8, (one per student)

Overview

Students now investigate the second differences in the areas of the leaves: These are differences between the differences.

About the Mathematics

In Section A, students found that for linear patterns, the first differences are equal for equal time differences. For quadratic relationships, the first differences are not equal, but the second differences are equal for equal steps in the table.

First and second differences are also discussed in the unit *Patterns and Figures*. The study of differences is named *differential calculus*. It is an intuitive preparation for the more formal mathematics of finding derivatives. In the *Mathematics in Context* curriculum, the study of differences is the endpoint of preparing for calculus. This lays a conceptual foundation for calculus at high school.

C Differences in Growth

Notes

7 This problem is critical. At this point students need to realize the common features of quadratic relationships.

After problem 8, you may want to have an in-depth class discussion about the previous problems. Discuss how the differences can be found and what they mean.

9a Discuss the usefulness of calculated leaf areas of 15.125 or 43.245. Ask, *Why isn't useful to give your answer to three decimal places? Why is it more appropriate to round?*

7. a. What is the value for A $(A = \frac{1}{2}h^2)$ if $h = 2\frac{1}{2}$?

b. How does the value of A for a poplar leaf change when you double the value of h? Use some specific examples to support your answer.

8. If the area of one poplar leaf is about 65 square centimeters (cm^2), what is its height? Explain how you found your answer.

The table shown below is also printed on **Student Activity Sheet 9**.

Height (in cm)	1	2	3	4	5	6	7	8
Area (in cm²)	0.5	2	4.5					

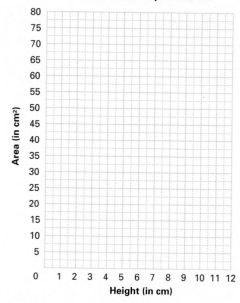

Area of Black Poplar Leaves

9. a. Use **Student Activity Sheet 9** to fill in the remaining area values in the table. Use this formula:

$$A = \frac{1}{2}h^2$$

b. Graph the formula on the grid. Why do you think the graph curves upward?

Assessment Pyramid

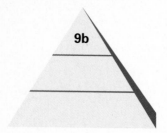

9b

Use algebraic models to represent realistic situations.

Reaching All Learners

Parent Involvement

After this page, you may ask students to tell family members what they have learned about differences in a table. This may inform parents about the *Mathematics in Context* approach toward developing concepts related to calculus.

Solutions and Samples

7. a. $A = \frac{1}{2} \times (2\frac{1}{2})^2 = \frac{1}{2} \times 6\frac{1}{4} = 3\frac{1}{8}$

b. When h is doubled, A is quadrupled. For example, if $h = 2$ cm, then
$A = \frac{1}{2} \times 4 = 2$ cm². If $h = 4$ cm, then
$A = \frac{1}{2} \times 16 = 8$ cm². Since $8 = 2 \times 4$,
the original area of 2cm² quadruples to 8 cm² when the height is doubled.

8. Its height is about 11.4 cm. Students can use the formula $A = \frac{1}{2} h^2$; if $A = 65$, then $h^2 = 130$, and $h = \sqrt{130} \approx 11.4$ cm.

9. a.

Height (in cm)	1	2	3	4	5	6	7	8
Area (in cm²)	0.5	2	4.5	8	12.5	18	24.5	32

b. Sample graph:

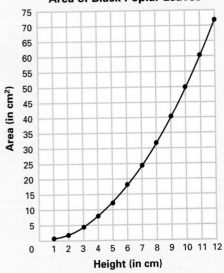

Area of Black Poplar Leaves

The graph curves upward because the area increases by a larger amount with each change in height.

Hints and Comments

Materials
Student Activity Sheet 9 (one per student).

Overview
Students continue investigating second differences in a table representing a quadratic relationship. They graph the formula for the area of a leaf and use the graph to estimate areas of leaves with given heights.

About the Mathematics
The formula for the area of a leaf is quadratic. In a quadratic formula, when the x-value is doubled, the resulting value quadruples. This can be explained with square diagrams. If the length of a side is doubled, the resulting square is the size of four of the original squares.

Comments About the Solutions
8. Students should be able to use tables, formulas, and graphs to find one value when given another.

Differences in Growth

Notes

c. Using your graph, estimate the areas of poplar leaves with the following heights: 5.5 cm, 9.3 cm, and 11.7 cm.

d. Check your answers to part **c**, using the formula for the area of a poplar leaf. Which method do you prefer for finding the area of a poplar leaf given its height: the graph or the formula? Explain.

If the second differences in the table are equal, the growth is **quadratic**.

Water Lily

The *Victoria regina*, named after Queen Victoria of England, is a very large water lily that grows in South America. The name was later changed to *Victoria amazonica*. The leaf of this plant can grow to nearly 2 meters (m) in diameter.

10 This problem reviews students' general knowledge of measurements. For example, the height of a door is approximately 2 m. The height of a grown person is usually less than 2 m, etc. These measurements are used as reference points for estimations.

10. How many of these full-grown leaves would fit on the floor of your classroom without overlapping?

Suppose you investigated the growth of a *Victoria amazonica* leaf and drew the following pictures on graph paper, one for every week.

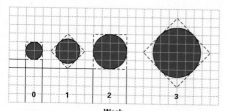

Week

11. How can you tell that the radius of the leaf does not grow linearly? Use the pictures shown above.

Use **Student Activity Sheet 10** for problem 12.

12. a. Make a table showing the length of the radius (in millimeters) of the lily each week. Try to make the numbers as accurate as possible.

b. Use the *first* and *second* differences in the table to find the next two entries in the table.

c. What can you conclude about the growth of the radius of the water lily?

Assessment Pyramid

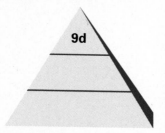

9d

Recognize the power of graphs and tables for solving problems.

Reaching All Learners

English Language Learners

Have students explain the difference between a radius and diameter, and model how to label each on an overhead transparency of **Student Activity Sheet 10**.

Advanced Learners

Have students try to compute the radius of each water lily without using a ruler. Finding the radii for weeks 1 and 3 requires some insight. Some students might recognize they can apply the Pythagorean theorem in this situation. Since a diagonal of each square in the grid is length $\sqrt{2}$, the radius of week 1 is $\sqrt{2}$ and the radius of week 3 is $2\sqrt{2}$.

Solutions and Samples

9. c. height 5.5 cm   area about 15 cm²

       height 9.3 cm   area about 43 cm²

       height 11.7 cm   area about 68 cm²

Allow a reasonable range for the answers of the area because students have to read them from the graph.

d. Discuss answers in class. Some students may prefer the graph because they can just read off the estimated values without doing any calculations. Others may prefer to have the exact calculations by using the formula.

10. Estimates will vary, depending on the size and layout of your classroom.

11. Answers will vary. Some students may say that they can tell from the differences in sizes of the leaf that the radius does not grow the same amount every week.

12. a. Tables will vary. Sample table:

Week	0	1	2	3
Radius (in mm)	5	7	10	14

b. Answers will vary, depending on the tables students made. Sample response:

first differences: 2, 3, 4, so the next two are 5 and 6

second differences: 1

The next two entries in the table are:

Week	0	1	2	3	4	5
Radius (in mm)	5	7	10	14	19	25

c. The growth is not linear (the first differences are not equal). The growth of the radius of the water lily is quadratic because the second differences in the table are equal.

Hints and Comments

Materials

centimeter rulers, (one per student);
Student Activity Sheet 10 (one per student)
transparency of Student Activity Sheet 10 (optional)

Overview

Students investigate the growth pattern of the radius of a water lily. They compare the lily's radius at different growth stages to determine whether or not the growth pattern is linear or quadratic.

About the Mathematics

The shape of the water lily leaf used here approximates the general shape of a circle. Therefore the pictures can be used to represent a growth model in a realistic situation.

Comments About the Solutions

9. d. Students may have different preferences. It takes less time to estimate from the graph, but the formula gives more precise values.

Notes

You may need to review the concept of area and remind students that area is measured in square units

Read and discuss with students the text and diagrams about how to reallot the area of a circle.

Briefly review students' solutions and strategies for these problems, focusing especially on problems 13c and 14b. Review that $r \times r$ can be written as "r squared," using an exponent.

14b If students are having difficulty, you may suggest that they look at the first and second differences.

The area of the leaves of *Victoria amazonica* is more important than the length of the radius if you want to compare the sizes of leaves while they grow. The following series of pictures shows one way of approximating the area of a circle if you know the radius.

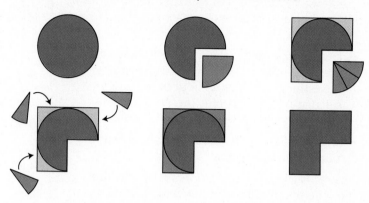

Using these pictures, you can show that if a circle has a radius of five units, the area is about 75 square units.

13. a. Explain how the pictures show the area is about 75 square units.

   b. Describe how you can find the area of a circle if you know its radius is ten units.

   c. Describe how you can find the area of any circle if you know the radius.

To find the area of a circle, you can use the general rule you found in the previous problem. The formula below is more accurate:

area of a circle $= \pi \times r \times r$, or

area of a circle $\approx 3.14 \times r \times r$, where r is the radius of the circle

14. a. Use the answers you found in problem 12. Make a new table showing the area of the leaves of the water lily each week.

   b. Does the area of the leaves show linear or quadratic growth? Explain your answer.

Assessment Pyramid

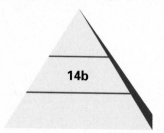

14b

Reason about situations of growth in terms of slope and increase.

Reaching All Learners

Hands-On Learning

Have students draw and cut out the pictures represented on this page on graph paper to enhance their understanding of the relationship between the area of the original circle and the area of the square.

Extension

Ask, *What is the area of a circle with a radius of 1, 2, 4, 8, 16, 32 in.?* Set up this problem as a table.

Radius	1	2	4	8	....
Area	....				

Ask, *What is the relationship between the radius and the area in the table?*

Solutions and Samples

13. a. The radius is the length of the side of a small square. Since each square has sides of 5 units, they each have areas of 25 square units ($5 \times 5 = 25$ square units). Since there are 3 squares (that represent the area of the one circle), the area of the circle is about 75 square units ($3 \times 25 = 75$ square units).

Another explanation: The area of the square is $10 \times 10 = 100$; the shaded part is $\frac{3}{4}$ of this, or 75.

b. If the radius is 10 units, the area is $100 \times 3 = 300$ square units.

c. If you know the radius of the circle, you can find the area by multiplying the radius by itself and then multiplying that product by three.

14. a. Tables will vary since the radius was measured by the students. Sample table:

Week	0	1	2	3
Area (in mm²)	78.5	153.9	314	615.4

b. first differences: 75.5; 160; 301

second differences: 84.5; 141

The growth is neither linear nor quadratic.

Note: You may want to use an estimated 3 instead of 3.14 in the formula

Area of a Circle $\approx 3 \times r \times r$

or you may remind your students of the use of π.

Hints and Comments

Materials

calculators (one per student);

Overview

Students review the formula for the area of a circle within the context of water lily leaves.

About the Mathematics

The conventional formula for the area of a circle is often better understood when the circle's area is visually "reallotted" to make three squares, each with sides equal to the circle's radius. Students may recall this strategy from the unit *Reallotment*. Students are also formally introduced to the formulas for area and perimeter of a circle, using π, in that unit.

Planning

Students may work in pairs or in small groups on problems 13 and 14.

Comments About the Solutions

13. a. You may make a drawing of this circle on the board or overhead projector and demonstrate how the circle's area can be reallotted to make three squares. You may need to explain how the picture of the three squares can be represented using the formula $A = 3 \times r \times r$. The 3 refers to the 3 squares, and $r \times r$ refers to the area of each square. Since the circle's wedges do not make an exact fit in the spaces, the formula $A = 3 \times r \times r$ is an approximation of the conventional formula, $A = \pi \times r \times r$.

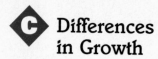

Differences in Growth

Notes

Encourage students to organize the information in a table before answering problem 15.

15a Ask. *If the weed did grow linearly, how much would it grow each year? (200 km²)*

Aquatic Weeds

The waterweed *Salvinia auriculata,* found in Africa, is a fast-growing weed. In 1959, a patch of *Salvinia auriculata* was discovered in Lake Kariba on the border of what are now Zimbabwe and Zambia. People noticed it was growing very rapidly.

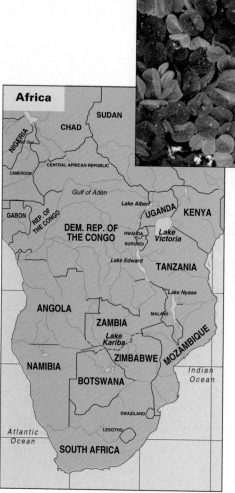

The first time it was measured, in 1959, it covered 199 square kilometers (km²). A year later, it covered about 300 km². In 1963, the weed covered 1,002 km² of the lake.

15. **a.** Did the area covered by the weed grow linearly? Explain.

   b. Was the growth quadratic? Explain.

Solutions and Samples

15. a. No. Explanations will vary. Sample responses:

- The first year the area increased by about 100 km². If it grew linearly, it would have grown this same amount every year. But we are told that in 1963 the weed covered 1,002 km², so the weed did not grow linearly.

- From 1959 to 1963 (in four years), the area increased by about 1,000 − 200 = 800 km². So if the area increased linearly, it would have increased by 800 ÷ 4 = 200 km² per year. But from 1959 to 1960, the area increased from 199 to 300 km², and that difference is not 200 km².

b. The growth is not quadratic. Sample answer:

Suppose the growth was quadratic, the table would look like this:

Week	1959	1960	1961	1962	1963
Area (in km²)	199	300	500	800	1,200

first differences: 100   200   300   400

second differences   100   100   100

Hints and Comments

Overview

Students investigate the growth of the area in a lake that is covered by a fast-growing weed.

About the Mathematics

The context of a growing weed informally introduces students to the concept of exponential growth. While linear growth can be identified by looking for equal increases over equal time periods, exponential growth is identified differently. In both growth-pattern situations, equal time periods must be considered.

Planning

You might want to read and discuss the text with students. They may solve problem 15 in small groups. Be sure to discuss students' solutions and strategies for this problem and read the text above problem 15.

Comments About the Solutions

15. Students should realize that the growth rate between the given years is not equal. You may suggest that they use a table, as shown, to see whether or not the growth amounts can be derived from the growth rate of the area between any two given years.

Week	1959	1960	1963
Area (in km²)	199	300	1,002

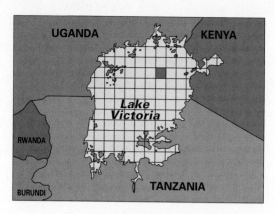

Lake Victoria is about 1,000 miles north of Lake Kariba. Suppose a different weed were found there.

Here is a map of Lake Victoria with a grid pattern drawn on it. One square of this grid is colored in to represent the area covered by the weed in one year.

16 By coloring the square units in the area, students will realize that the total number of squares they have colored at the end of the current year is equal to the number they will color next year. This prepares students to later write a recursive formula to describe this exponential growth situation.

Make sure students understand the term *growth factor*.

Use **Student Activity Sheet 11** to answer problems 16–19.

Suppose the area of the weeds in Lake Victoria doubles every year.

16. If the shaded square represents the area currently covered by the weed, how many squares would represent the area covered next year? A year later? A year after that?

Angela shows the growth of the area covered by the weed by coloring squares on the map. She uses a different color for each year. She remarks, "The number of squares I color for a certain year is exactly the same as the number already colored for all of the years before."

17. Use **Student Activity Sheet 11** to show why Angela is or is not correct.

18. How many years would it take for the lake to be about half covered?

19. How many years would it take for the lake to be totally covered?

Double Trouble

Carol is studying a type of bacteria at school. Bacteria usually reproduce by cell division. During cell division, a bacterium splits in half and forms two new bacteria. Each bacterium then splits again, and so on. These bacteria are said to have a **growth factor** of two because their amount doubles after each time period.

Reaching All Learners

Intervention

Some students may have difficulty with the concept of doubling in problem 17. They may use the following incorrect reasoning: *There are 8 squares colored this year. Double that and you get 16, so I need to color 16 new squares.* Instead, they should make sure they have colored enough new squares to match the total number of squares that will be covered by weeds at the end of each year.

Solutions and Samples

16. Next year: two squares

A year later: four squares

A year after that: eight squares

17. Angela is correct. Sample explanations:

In one year, there are 8 squares covered. The next year, that number will double to make 16 squares covered. So you need to color 8 additional squares.

To double something, you add that amount to itself ($2 \times$ area = area + area).

Using the map:

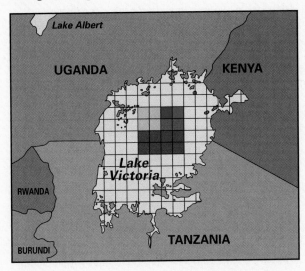

18. It would take between five and six years for the lake to be half covered. Sample explanation:

The lake covers an area of 100 square units. After five years, 32 square units would be covered, and after six years, 64 square units would be covered. So it would take somewhere between five and six years for the lake to be half covered.

19. It would take between six and seven years for the lake to be fully covered. Explanations will vary. Sample explanation:

The lake covers an area of 100 square units. After six years, 64 square units would be covered, and after seven years, more than 100 square units would be covered. So it would take somewhere between six and seven years for the lake to be fully covered.

Hints and Comments

Materials

Student Activity Sheet 11 (one per student); colored pencils (one box per group)

Overview

Students use a map to investigate the area of weed growth on a lake over a time span.

About the Mathematics

By the end of this section, students should understand the basis for exponential growth used in this section, doubling. They should be able to look at doubling patterns in two different ways, as shown below.

To find the area for the fourth year, take the area of the current year (8) and add the same amount:

$8 + 8 = 16$ square units.

Year	0	1	2	3	4
Area (squared)	1	2	4	8	16

+ 1   + 2   + 4   + 8

This leads to the formula

NEXT = CURRENT + CURRENT.

Another way to find the area for the fourth year is to take the previous year's area and multiply it by two: $2 \times 8 = 16$ square units.

This leads to the formula:

Year	0	1	2	3	4
Area (squared)	1	2	4	8	16

$\times 2$ $\times 2$ $\times 2$ $\times 2$

NEXT = $2 \times$ CURRENT

A formal discussion about these recursive formulas is not necessary at this point.

Planning

Students may work on problems 16–19 in pairs or in small groups. Be sure to discuss students' solutions and strategies for these problems.

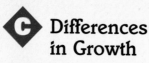

Differences in Growth

Notes

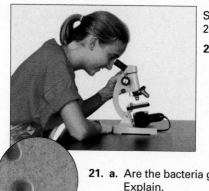

Suppose the number of bacteria doubles every 20 minutes.

20. Starting with a single bacterium, calculate the number of existing bacteria after two hours and 40 minutes. Make a table like the one below to show your answer.

Time (in minutes)	0	20	40
Number of Bacteria			

21. **a.** Are the bacteria growing linearly or in a quadratic pattern? Explain.

b. Extend the table to graph the differences in the number of bacteria over the course of two hours and 40 minutes.

c. Describe the graph.

22. **Reflect** How will the table and the graph in problem 21 change if the growth factor is four instead of two?

Two thousand bacteria are growing in the corner of the kitchen sink. You decide it is time to clean your house. You use a cleanser on the sink that is 99% effective in killing bacteria.

23. How many bacteria survive your cleaning?

24. If the number of bacteria doubles every 20 minutes, how long will it take before there are as many bacteria as before?

25. Find a NEXT-CURRENT formula for the growth of the bacteria.

This type of growth, where each new value is found by multiplying the previous number by a growth factor, is called **exponential growth**.

Time (in hours)	0	1	2	3
Number of Bacteria	1	6	36	216

× 6   × 6   × 6

21 Students might have difficulty in using an appropriate scale for the axes. Be sure to discuss the idea that the graph shows that doubling results in an increasing growth rate.

22 Make sure students understand that the term *growth factor* refers to multiplication and not additive growth.

22 You may ask students how they might find a more precise answer to this problem. Some students might suggest using a graph.

Assessment Pyramid

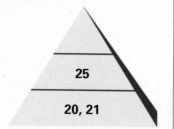

25

20, 21

Describe exponential growth with recursive formulas.

Identify patterns from a table and graph

Reaching All Learners

Vocabulary Building

Remind students of the term *scale factor* from the unit *Ratio and Rates*. Have students explain what *factor* means in their own words. Highlight student responses that recognize the relationship between factors and multiplication; for example, "factors are numbers you multiply together to get another number."

Solutions and Samples

20. After 2 hours and 40 minutes, or 160 minutes, there are 256 bacteria.

Time (in minutes)	0	20	40	60	80	100	120	140	160
Number of Bacteria	1	2	4	8	16	32	64	128	256

21. a. No. The bacteria are not growing in a linear pattern. Explanations will vary. Sample explanation:

If you calculate the differences, you will see that the number of bacteria is not increasing by equal amounts.

Time (in minutes)	0	20	40	60
Number of Bacteria	1	2	4	8

+ 1   + 2   + 4

The bacteria are not growing in a quadratic pattern. If you look at the second differences in the table, you can see they are not equal.

b.

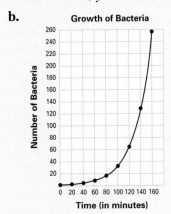

Growth of Bacteria

c. Descriptions will vary. Sample description:

The graph is not a straight line. It becomes steeper and steeper, showing that the number is increasing faster and faster.

22. Table:

Time (in minutes)	0	20	40	60
Number of Bacteria	1	4	16	64

Graph:

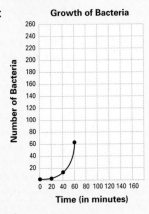

Growth of Bacteria

Hints and Comments

Materials

graph paper (one sheet per student)

Overview

Students are introduced to the concept of a growth factor. They use the given growth factor to solve problems about the growth of bacteria.

About the Mathematics

Exponential growth can be modeled with repeated multiplication. In the table below, the multiplication factor (× 2) is the ratio between the two numbers for adjoining time periods. In exponential patterns, this multiplication factor is known as the *growth factor*. Some students may remember the term *factor of enlargement* from the unit *Ratios and Rates*. Use this term to help reinforce the idea that a factor deals with the operation of multiplication.

Planning

Read and discuss the text on Student Book, page 31, together. Students may work on problems 20 and 21 individually or in small groups. These problems may also be used as informal assessment. Problems 22 and 23 may be assigned as homework.

Comments About the Solutions

20. Some students may arrive at the incorrect answer of 16 by using the following table.

× 2

Time (in minutes)	0	20	40	80	160
Number of Bacteria	1	2	4	8	16

× 2

23. There will be 20 bacteria left. Students may reason that 99% are killed, so 1% survive, and 1% of 2,000 is 20.

24. Between 120 and 140 minutes. Some students may use a table to find the answer. Sample table:

Time (in minutes)	0	20	40	60	80	100	120	140
Number of Bacteria	20	40	80	160	320	640	1,280	2,560

25. NEXT = CURRENT × 2

**Differences
in Growth**

Notes

The Summary for this
section reiterates each of
the various strategies for
using table differences to
identify growth as linear,
quadratic, or exponential.
Be sure to go through the
Summary carefully. It is
critical that students
understand the difference
between quadratic and
exponential growth.

 Differences in Growth

Summary

Growth can be described by a table, a graph, or an equation.
If you look at differences in a table, you know that:

- if the first differences are equal, the growth is linear. The rate of
  change is constant. In the table, the height of a plant is measured
  each week, and each week the same length is added to the
  previous length.

Time (in weeks)	0	1	2	3	4	5
Height (in cm)	10	15	20	25	30	35

+5 +5 +5 +5 +5

- if the first differences are not equal but the second differences are
  equal, the growth is quadratic.

In the table it shows the relationship between length and area of
squares. If the length increases by 1 cm each time, the "second
differences" are equal.

Length of Square (in cm)	1	2	3	4	5	6
Surface Area of Square (in cm^2)	1	4	9	16	25	36

+3 +5 +7 +9 +11

+2 +2 +2 +2

Reaching All Learners

Parent Involvement

Have parents review the section with their child to relate the Check Your
Work problems to the problems from the section.

Hints and Comments

Overview

Students review different types of growth by looking at tables.

Writing Opportunity

Have students add to the Summary by writing about graphs that represent the different types of growth. They may use the tables shown in the Summary to draw graphs.

Planning

After finishing Section C, you may assign problems for extra practice from the Additional Practice section on pages 50 and 51 of the Student Book.

The table below shows that the area of a weed is being measured yearly and that the weed has a growth factor of two. Notice that having a growth factor of two means that the area covered by the weed is doubling every year.

Year	1	2	3	4	5
Area (in km²)	400	800	1,600	3,200	6,400

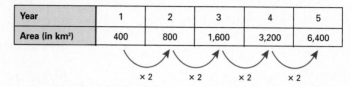

$\times 2 \quad \times 2 \quad \times 2 \quad \times 2$

- if each value in the table is found by multiplying by a **growth factor**, the growth is **exponential**.

Check Your Work

Consider the following formula for the area of a leaf: $A = \frac{1}{3}h^2$

Height (h) is measured in centimeters; area (A) is measured in square centimeters.

1. a. Use the formula for the area of a leaf to fill in the missing values in the table.

h (in cm)	3	4	5		7	8
A (in cm²)				12		

   b. Is the growth linear, quadratic, or exponential? Why?

The next table shows a model for the growth of dog nails.

Time (in months)	0	1	2	3	4	5
Length (in mm)	15	15.5	16	16.5	17	17.5

2. a. How can you be sure the growth represented in the table is linear?

   b. What is the increase in length of the dog nail per month?

Assessment Pyramid

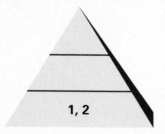

1, 2

Assesses Section C Goals

Reaching All Learners

Extension

To reinforce the relationship between patterns and growth factors, ask, *To double a number what can you do?* (Multiply by 2.) This is a growth factor of 2. *To triple a number what can you do?* (Multiply by 3.) This is a growth factor of 3.

Solutions and Samples

Answers to Check Your Work

1. a. Remember that squaring a number goes before multiplying. An example, for $h = 4$:

$A = \frac{1}{3} \times (4^2) = \frac{1}{3} \times 4 \times 4 = \frac{16}{3}$

$A = 5\frac{1}{3}$ (Note that you should always write fractions in simplest form and change improper fractions to mixed numbers.)

h (in cm)	3	4	5	6	7	8
A (in cm²)	3	$5\frac{1}{3}$	$8\frac{1}{3}$	12	$16\frac{1}{3}$	$21\frac{1}{3}$

b. The first differences are: $2\frac{1}{3}$, 3, $3\frac{2}{3}$, $4\frac{1}{3}$, and 5; the growth is not linear because the first differences in the table are not equal. The second differences are: $\frac{2}{3}$, $\frac{2}{3}$, $\frac{2}{3}$, and $\frac{2}{3}$, the growth is quadratic because the second differences are equal.

The growth is not exponential because the numbers in the second row are not multiplied by the same number to get from one to the next.

2. a. The first differences in the table are equal; they are 0.5. Therefore, you know the growth is linear.

b. The increase in length of the dog's nail each month is 0.5 mm.

Hints and Comments

Overview

Students use the Check Your Work problems as self-assessment. The answers to these problems are provided in the Student Book.

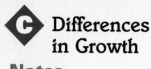

Use this formula for the next problem:

area of a circle ≈ 3.14 × *r* × *r*, where *r* is the radius of the circle

3. **a.** Find the area of a circle with the radius 2.5. You may use a calculator.

   b. How many decimal places did you use for your answer? Explain why you used this number of decimal places.

   c. Find the radius of a circle if the area is 100 cm². You may use a calculator. Show your calculations.

Suppose that you are offered a job for a six-month period and that you are allowed to choose how you will be paid:

$1,000 every week   or   1 cent the first week,
2 cents the second week,
4 cents the third week,
8 cents the fourth week,
and so on…

4. Which way of being paid would you choose? Why?

For Further Reflection

From birth to age 14, children grow taller. Think about your own growth during that time and describe whether you think it is linear, quadratic, exponential, or other. Give specific examples.

For Further Reflection

The reflection question is meant to summarize and extend what students have learned in the section.

Assessment Pyramid

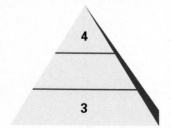

Assesses Section C Goals

Reaching All Learners

Writing Opportunity

Problem 4, which many students find challenging, is a classic problem that compares additive and exponential growth. Have students write in their notebooks about which choice they would make and why.

Solutions and Samples

3. a. $3.14 \times 2.5 \times 2.5 \approx 19.6$

Area of the circle is about 19.6.

Note that in the given radius of 2.5, no units were mentioned.

b. You may have noted that the answer 19.625 was shown in the calculator window.

However, because the radius is given in one decimal, the answer should also be in one decimal.

c. If you do not have a calculator, try some carefully chosen examples.

You know that $3 \times 25 = 75$, so $r > 5$.

$3 \times 36 = 108$, so $r < 6$; you now know that r is between 5 and 6.

Try $r = 5.5$.
$3.14 \times 5.5 \times 5.5 \approx 95$ (too little)

Try $r = 5.6$.
$3.14 \times 5.6 \times 5.6 \approx 98$ (too little)

Try $r = 5.7$.
$3.14 \times 5.7 \times 5.7 \approx 102$ (too much)

The answer will be $r \approx 5.6$ or $r \approx 5.7$.

Using a calculator:

$3.14 \times r \times r = 100$

$r \times r = 100 \div 3.14 = 31.847\dots$ (Don't round off until you have the final answer.)

Find a number that gives 31.84…. as a result if squared. Or:
The square root ($\sqrt{\ }$) of 31.847…. is about 5.6.

Radius r is about 5.6.

4. Discuss your answer with a classmate. Sample calculations:

Doubling a penny adds up to more money in a six-month period than receiving $1,000 a week. I calculated how much money I would make after six months, using the first case:
26 weeks × $1,000 per week = $26,000.

For the second case, I calculated the amount I would receive week by week with a calculator:

In week ten, the amount would be $5.12, and all together I would have been paid $10.23.

In week twenty, the amount I would make would already be $5,242.88, and the total I would have earned would be $10,485.75.

After 23 weeks, my pay for one week would already be $41,943.04, so for that one week I would make more than I would in six months in the first case. So I would choose the doubling method.

Hints and Comments

Overview

Students use the Check Your Work problems as self-assessment. The answers to these problems are provided in the Student Book.

Comments About the Problems

Problem 4 of the Check Your Work section is a classic problem.

Remembering that in the second way I have to find how much I would make each week and add up what I was already paid, in week 22, I would have made $20,971.52. My total earnings after that week would be $41,943.03. So the doubling method is better.

For Further Reflection

Answers will vary. Students should recognize that growth is often erratic. While there may be brief periods where growth appears to jump faster and faster—a teenage "growth spurt"—between ages 2 and 7, growth might appear to be linear. In their response, it is more important that students are able to give correct examples for how they choose to describe their growth.

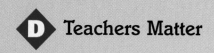

Section Focus

Section D introduces the terms *cycle* and *period* to describe features of a periodic phenomenon. Periodic graphs are investigated within the context of tides, temperature changes in an air-conditioned room, blood pressure, and laps on a racetrack.

Pacing and Planning

Day 12: Fishing		Student pages 35–37
INTRODUCTION	Problems 1–3	Draw a simple graph to show how water levels in the ocean change over time.
CLASSWORK	Problems 4 and 5	Interpret and create a tidal graph that represents the change in water level in tidal regions.
HOMEWORK	Problems 6 and 7	Compare tidal graphs and describe the changes in water level.

Day 13: The Air Conditioner		Student pages 38–39
INTRODUCTION	Problems 8 and 9	Interpret a graph representing temperature changes in an air-conditioned room.
CLASSWORK	Problems 10–12	Identify the period and label one cycle in a periodic graph.
HOMEWORK	Problems 13–15	Read and interpret a periodic graph.

Day 14: Summary		Student pages 40–42
INTRODUCTION	Review homework.	Review homework from Day 13.
CLASSWORK	Check Your Work	Student self-assessment: Create and interpret periodic graphs.
ASSESSMENT	Quiz 2	Assesses Section C and D Goals.

Additional Resources: *Algebra Tools*; Additional Practice, Section D, page 51

Materials

Student Resources

Quantities listed are per student.

- **Student Activity Sheets 12 and 13**

Teachers Resources

No resources required.

Student Materials

Quantities listed are per pair of students, unless otherwise noted.

- Calculator
- Colored pencils, one box
- Graph paper (four sheets per student)

* See Hints and Comments for optional materials.

Learning Lines

Discern Different Types of Graphs

In Section A, students investigated a variety of graphs. In this section, a new type of graph is introduced, the periodic graph.

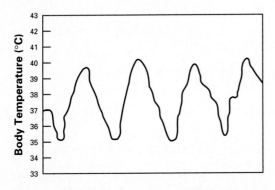

Students interpret and draw a tidal graph that represents the change in water level in tidal regions. They describe the increase and decrease of the temperature in an air-conditioned room and identify the period and cycle of several periodic graphs. They do not use formulas and/or tables that describe periodic phenomena.

At the End of the Section: Learning Outcomes

Students identify the characteristics of a periodic graph and are able to identify the cycle and period in a periodic graph.

 Cycles

Fishing

Camilla and Lewis are fishing in the ocean. Their boat is tied to a post in the water. Lewis is bored because the fish are not biting, so he decides to amuse himself by keeping track of changes in the water level due to the tide.

He makes a mark on the post every 15 minutes. He made the first mark (at the top) at 9:00 A.M.

1. What do the marks tell you about the way the water level is changing?

2. Make a graph that shows how the water level changed during this time.

3. What can you say about how the graph will continue? (Think about the tides of the ocean.) You don't need to graph it.

Reaching All Learners

Extension

Ask students to bring in some sample charts of tide information. A search on the Internet for "tide charts" will indicate many options for information. Students may also want to explore how the sun and moon influence ocean tides day to day and throughout the year.

Solutions and Samples

1. Answers will vary. Sample responses:
   The water level is going down more and more.

   The water level is decreasing at a faster and faster rate.

2.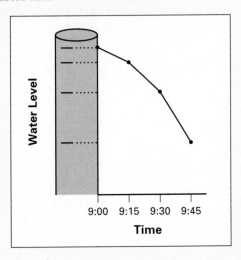

3. Answers will vary. Students' responses should indicate that the graph may continue downward for a number of hours and then eventually begin to rise. Some students may say that the graph will repeat the same pattern over time.

Hints and Comments

Materials

graph paper (optional, one sheet per student)

Overview

Students use marks on a post to draw a graph that shows how the water level changes over time.

About the Mathematics

The marks on the post showing the differences in water height are similar to the marks on the door and the core samples of Section A. They all show a pattern of change over time. Note that the marks on the post here indicate a change in the rate of decrease.

The context of this page—the change of water level, which is influenced by the tides—also produces continuous graphs. Because tide phenomena are periodic events, the graphs also show a regular, repetitive pattern.

Planning

Students may work on problems 1–3 in pairs or in small groups. Be sure to discuss students' solutions and strategies for these problems.

Comments About the Solutions

1. Make sure that students realize that the marks on the post were made consecutively from top to bottom.

2. Some students may trace the marks from the post (from Student Book page 35) on the edge of a strip of paper and use this strip to draw the four points of the graph. The points of the graph can then be connected. See the Solutions and Samples column. Some students may want to use graph paper to draw the graph.

Notes

Ask students whether or not these tidal graphs tell anything about the depths of the water.

It is important to discuss whether or not this graph could have a vertical line for one section. Ask students what it would mean to have a vertical line in the graph. (This would mean that the water level dropped or rose a certain number of centimeters in zero seconds.)

4 Students can easily find the times when it is safe to walk on the tide flats by drawing a horizontal line on the tidal graph.

D Cycles

High Tide, Low Tide

During low tide naturalists lead hikes along coastal tide flats. They point out the various plant and animal species that live in this unique environment. Some of the plants and animals hikers see on the walk are seaweed, oystercatchers, curlews, plovers, mussels, jellyfish, and seals.

Walkers do not always stay dry during the walk; sometimes the water may even be waist-high. Walkers carry dry clothing in their backpacks and wear tennis shoes to protect their feet from shells and sharp stones.

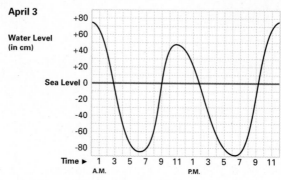

April 3

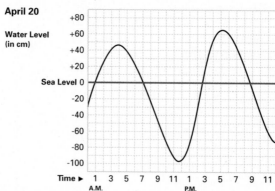

April 20

The graphs show the tides for the tide flats for two days in April. Walking guides recommend that no one walk in water deeper than 45 cm above the lowest level of the tide.

4. When is it safe to walk on the tide flats on these two days in April?

Reaching All Learners

Accommodation

You might want to make a transparency of the tidal graphs shown on Student Book page 36 and have some students use the overhead projector to show how they used the graphs to solve problem 4.

Intervention

If students have difficulty starting problem 4, ask, *Where on the graph is the lowest level of the tide?* (6:30 P.M. for April 3 and 11:30 A.M. for April 20.) *Where is the water 45 cm above the lowest level?* (All points at −43 cm for April 3 and at −50 cm for April 20.)

Solutions and Samples

4. The times it would be safe to walk along the beaches are:

April 3: from about 3:45 A.M. until about 8:20 A.M. (about 4.5 hours) and from about 3:15 P.M. until about 8:30 P.M. (about 5.25 hours)

April 20: from about 9:15 A.M. until about 1:45 P.M. (about 4.5 hours), and again at about 10:15 P.M.

Note: The levels of low and high tides are different at different times.

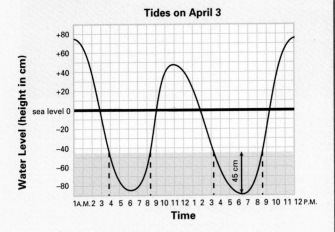

Tides on April 3

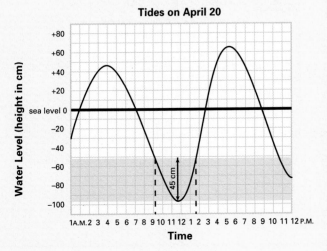

Tides on April 20

Hints and Comments

Materials

transparency of the tidal graphs on Student Book page 36 (optional, one per class);

Overview

Students interpret a tidal graph to solve a problem about walking along the shore.

Planning

You might read this page and complete problem 4 together as a whole-class activity.

Comments About the Solutions

4. The solution can be found by shading the section of the graph (or by drawing a horizontal line at a height) that is 45 cm above the lowest level of the tide. See the Solutions and Samples column.

Note: It is only safe to walk along the Dutch Shallows after sunrise; this area could be dangerous in the dark.

Notes

5 Students use the eight given points to draw a graph. The graph should not have sharp zigzag edges, since the water level increases and decreases gradually. Students' graphs will vary in precision and neatness.

5 Remind students that 12 A.M. is midnight and 12 P.M. is noon.

Golden Gate Bridge

In different parts of the world, the levels of high and low tides vary. The amount of time between the tides may also vary. Here is a tide schedule for the area near the Golden Gate Bridge in San Francisco, California.

5. Use the information in the table to sketch a graph of the water levels near the Golden Gate Bridge for these three days. Use **Student Activity Sheet 12** for your graph.

Date	Low	High
Aug. 7	2:00 A.M./12 cm 1:24 P.M./94 cm	9:20 A.M./131 cm 7:47 P.M./189 cm
Aug. 8	2:59 A.M./6 cm 2:33 P.M./94 cm	10:18 A.M./137 cm 8:42 P.M./189 cm
Aug. 9	3:49 A.M./0 cm 3:29 P.M./91 cm	11:04 A.M./143 cm 9:34 P.M./186 cm

6. Describe how the water level changed.

7. Compare your graph to the graphs on the previous page. What similarities and differences do you notice?

Reaching All Learners

Advanced Learners

If you live near bodies of water that have tidal fluctuations, you can obtain local times for high and low tides in the local newspaper. Students could then use this information to draw additional tidal graphs.

Writing Opportunity

Make available a sample graph of fluctuation in tides from the Internet or some other resource. Have students write a story to go along with the graph. Also encourage students to make a table from the graph that indicates the highs and lows for each day, in a format similar to the table shown in problem 5.

Solutions and Samples

5. Sample graph:

Tides at the Golden Gate Bridge

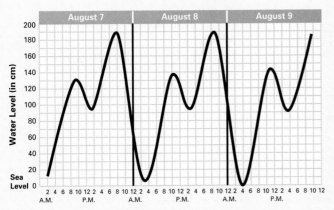

6. Answers will vary, and some descriptions may be more detailed than others. For example, students may include extensive information about times and heights. Sample responses:

On the first day, the tide rose for about seven hours, and at 9:20 A.M. it was high tide. Then it fell for about four hours. Then the tide rose again for about six hours. When high tide was reached at about 8:00 P.M., the level was higher than the high tide level in the morning. Then for the rest of the day, the tide fell. On the second and third days, the changes in the water level show the same pattern as on the first day.

There are two high and two low tides each day. It seems like the low tides are getting lower and the high tides are getting higher.

7. Answers will vary. Sample responses:

All the graphs show that there are two high tides and two low tides for each day. The difference is that in San Francisco, the water levels for the two high tides in a single day differ quite a bit. The same thing is true for water levels for the low tides. In the graphs of problem 5, the water levels for the high tides on a single day are almost the same.

The graph of the tides in San Francisco varies more than the graph of the coastal tide flats.

The water level in the tide flats changes from below sea level to above sea level; the water level in San Francisco is always at or above sea level.

Hints and Comments

Materials

Student Activity Sheet 12 (one per student); graph paper (one sheet per student)

Overview

Students use the data in a table about the times and levels of low tide and high tide to sketch a graph of the water level at the Golden Gate Bridge over a period of three days. Then they compare this graph with those on the previous page.

Planning

Students may work in pairs on problems 5–7. You may want students to finish these problems as homework.

Comments About the Solutions

Observe that no tidal graph shows curves like this.

(These graphs show three different water levels at the same time, which is impossible.)

To help students get started, discuss how to plot points for the first two hours of the day on August 7.

6. Students' answers should include a description of the two (relative) high tides and low tides on one day, and the repeating pattern.

7. Differences in water levels of high tides and low tides at the Golden Gate Bridge and the Dutch Shallows are due to the differences in the shapes of the coastlines near the two bodies of water.

Notes

By this point in the unit, students should be able to think about periodicity in terms of both the real-world context and the graph.

9a and **b** This is the first problem in which students must identify the period and cycle in a periodic graph. Point out that a graph's cycle can be colored at different places on the graph curve. Once one cycle is colored, it makes it easy to identify the period of the graph, the time interval along the horizontal axis that it takes to complete one cycle.

The Air Conditioner

Room Temperature

Suppose the graph on the left shows the temperature changes in an air-conditioned room.

8. Describe what is happening in the graph. Why do you think this is happening?

The graphs you have seen in this section have one thing in common: They have a shape that repeats. A repeating graph is called a **periodic graph**. The amount of time it takes for a periodic graph to repeat is called a **period** of the graph. The portion of the graph that repeats is called a **cycle**.

9. a. How long (in minutes) is a period in the above graph?

   b. On **Student Activity Sheet 13**, color one cycle on the graph.

Blood Pressure

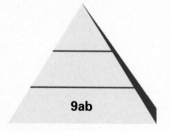

Your heart pumps blood throughout your system of arteries. When doctors measure blood pressure, they usually measure the pressure of the blood in the artery of the upper arm.

Your blood pressure is not constant. The graph on the right shows how blood pressure may change over time.

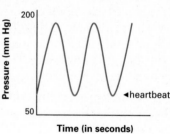

10. What can you tell about blood pressure just before a heartbeat?

11. What happens to blood pressure after a heartbeat?

12. Is this graph periodic? Explain your answer.

Assessment Pyramid

9ab

Identify characteristics of periodic graphs.

Reaching All Learners

Vocabulary Building

If students are having difficulty, you might draw a different example of a periodic graph and discuss the concepts of period and cycle with students.

Extension

You might discuss how the graph would change if the person had been running and the heartbeat was twice as fast.

Solutions and Samples

8. Answers will vary. Some students may comment that the temperature rises when the air conditioner is off and falls when it is on.

9. **a.** The period in the graph shown is 30 minutes.

   b. Answers will vary, depending on where a student starts to color a cycle. A cycle is correctly shown if it covers the time period that corresponds to students' answers for problem 9a.

10. Answers will vary. Sample response:

    The blood pressure is at its lowest point just before the heart beats.

11. Answers will vary. Sample response:

    After a heartbeat, the blood pressure rises rapidly, then rises more slowly, and finally stops rising. The pressure then begins to fall, slowly at first, then more rapidly, then more slowly again until it reaches its lowest value.

12. Yes, this is a periodic graph because the cycle repeats.

Hints and Comments

Materials

Student Activity Sheet 13 (one per student)

Overview

Students interpret a graph that shows a repeating pattern of temperature changes in an air-conditioned room. Students are introduced to a new context addressing a cyclic process, blood pressure. They investigate a graph that shows how blood pressure can change over time.

About the Mathematics

The concepts of a periodic graph, a period, and a cycle are made explicit on this page. Although these are new mathematical concepts, students may already have some understanding of periodic events, since repeating patterns are frequently found in science and nature. For example, sound and light waves show repeating patterns that can be illustrated using a periodic graph. High and low tides, phases of the moon, as well as the human heartbeat are also characterized by repeating patterns that make periodic graphs. Note that sometimes a phenomenon approximates a regular pattern but is not exactly periodic. In such cases, the periodic function serves as a model.

Planning

You may want students to work individually on problems 10–12.

Extension

You may have students work in pairs or small groups on the following activity.

1. Use a reference book or experiment to find the following information:

   • How many times do you inhale and exhale in one minute?

   • How much air do you inhale when you breathe normally?

   • What is the volume of your lungs?

2. Make a graph that shows the volume of your lungs over a time period of 15 seconds.

3. If your graph is periodic, how long is a period? If it is not periodic, explain why.

Notes

You may want to begin with a short discussion about the context, racetracks, and talk about graphs that show speed over time.

15 Some students may not recognize that the speed graph is periodic, since the graph would not continue to repeat forever. You may need to help students identify what one period is in this graph, the distance it takes to complete one cycle on the graph.

The Racetrack

A group of racecar drivers are at a track getting ready to practice for a big race. The drawing shows the racetrack as seen from above.

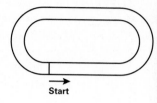

Start →

13. Make a sketch of the track in your notebook. Color it to show where the drivers should speed up and where they should slow down. Include a key to show the meanings of the colors or patterns you chose.

14. Make a graph of the speed of a car during three laps around the track. Label your graph like the one here.

Speed

Distance Along the Track

15. Explain why your graph is or is not periodic.

Assessment Pyramid

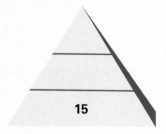

15

Identify characteristics of periodic graphs.

Reaching All Learners

Accommodation

If students have difficulty distinguishing between graphs that show distance over time and speed over time, you might want students to create a speed graph for a car ride with miles per hour on the vertical axis and times on the horizontal axis.

Act It Out

Have several students model the speed variation shown on their graph of the racetrack speed by walking around the classroom to match another student's narration of the information on the graph.

Solutions and Samples

13. Drawings will vary. Sample drawing:

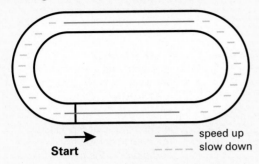

14. Answers will vary, but the graph should correspond with the colored parts of the track in problem 18. Sample response:

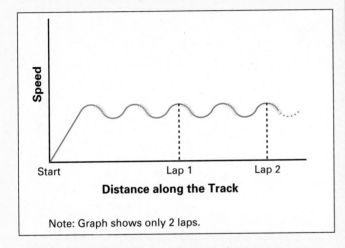

Note: Graph shows only 2 laps.

15. Explanations will vary. Sample explanation:

My graph is periodic. It shows a repeating pattern between some time after the beginning and the end of the race.

Hints and Comments

Materials

graph paper (one sheet per student)

Overview

Students sketch a racetrack to indicate where racecar drivers should speed up and slow down. They also make a graph that shows the speed of a racecar during three laps around the track.

About the Mathematics

The periodic graph on this page shows the speed of a car over time.

Planning

Students may work in pairs on problems 13–15. These are optional problems and may be omitted or assigned as homework if time is a concern.

Comments About the Solutions

13. The purpose of this problem is to get students to begin thinking about where a racecar driver will speed up or slow down before students actually make a graph showing the speed over time. In general, racecar drivers speed up halfway through the curved areas and on the straightaways. Racecars may be traveling at a constant speed at the end of the straightaways if the cars are being driven at their maximum speed.

14. Students may use the racetrack sketch they drew in the previous problem to help them make their speed graphs here.

Notes

You might discuss the Summary with the whole class as follows. Ask one student to draw an example of a periodic graph on the board. Then ask another student to explain why the graph is periodic. If the axes aren't labeled yet, you may ask a third student to label them. Another student can be asked to color a cycle, and yet another student can be asked to tell what one period is for the graph.

D Cycles

Summary

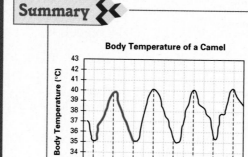

Body Temperature of a Camel

A *periodic graph* shows a repeating pattern. In real life, there can be small changes in the pattern.

A *period* on the graph is the length of time or the distance required to complete one *cycle*, or the part of the pattern that is repeated. One cycle is indicated on the graph; the period is 24 hours, or one day.

Check Your Work

The graph shows the height of the seawater near the port of Hoeck in the Netherlands.

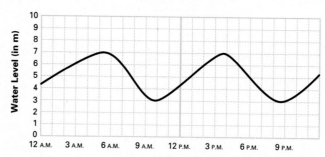

Tidal Graph for One Day

1. **a.** Is this graph a periodic graph? Why?

   b. How many hours after the start of this graph was low tide?

   c. What is the depth of the water during low tide?

   d. How many hours pass between two high tides?

   e. What is the period?

Assessment Pyramid

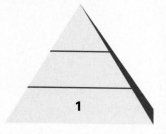

Assesses Section D Goals

Reaching All Learners

Parent Involvement

Have parents review the section with their child to relate the Check Your Work problems to the problems from the section.

Writing Opportunity

Have students make up their own graph and a "race story" that describes the critical events in the race.

Solutions and Samples

Answers to Check Your Work

1. **a.** The graph is periodic; the same pattern is repeated.

   b. After about ten hours (or a little less than ten hours).

   c. During low tide, the depth of the water is 3 m.

   d. Ten hours pass between two high tides.

   e. The period is one full cycle, so ten hours.

Hints and Comments

Overview

Students read and discuss the Summary, which reviews the main concepts of this section. They use the Check Your Work problems as self-assessment. The answers to these problems are provided in the Student Book.

Planning

After finishing Section D, you may assign problems for extra practice from the Additional Practice section on page 51 of the Student Book.

Notes

2a You may want to have students mark several key parts of the graph with a label that relates the behavior in the graph to what is happening to the refrigerator. *When does it turn on? When does it shut off?*

In a refrigerator, the temperature is not always the same. Even if the door is closed all the time, the temperature will slowly rise. In some refrigerators, as soon as the temperature reaches 45°F, the refrigeration system starts to work. The temperature will decrease until it reaches 35°F. In general, this takes about 10 minutes. Then the temperature starts rising again until it reaches 45°F. This takes about 20 minutes. Then the whole cycle starts all over again.

2. **a.** Draw a graph that fits the above information about the refrigeration system. Make your graph as accurately as possible. Be sure to label the axes.

   b. How many minutes does one complete cycle take?

Three periodic graphs are shown.

3. Which graph shows a situation that has a period of about six? Explain your reasoning.

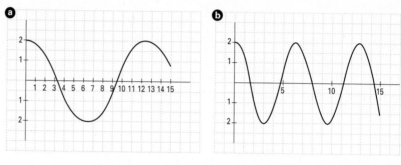

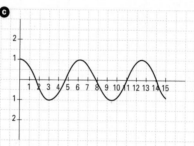

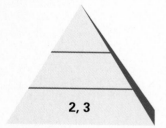
Reaching All Learners

Extension

Challenge students to draw another periodic graph (using their own racetrack design) showing three laps in which the following events occurred:

Lap One: The racecar got a flat tire halfway into the first straightaway, causing it to slow down to a crawl, make a pit stop to change the flat tire, and reenter the race at the beginning of the first curve.

Lap Two: The racecar encountered no problems during this lap.

Lap Three: The racecar did not slow down enough as it approached the second curve, causing it to spin out of control. The car came to a complete stop, then proceeded to continue the race.

Solutions and Samples

2. a.

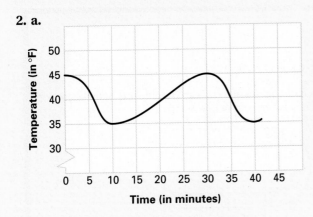

b. One complete cycle takes 30 minutes.

3. Graphs **b** and **c** have a period of about six. Note that the period of graph **a** is about 12.5.

Overview

Students use the Check Your Work problems as self-assessment. The answers to these problems are provided in the Student Book.

Planning

After finishing Section D, you may assign problems for extra practice from the Additional Practice section on page 51 of the Student Book.

Notes

For Further Reflection

The reflection question is meant to summarize and extend what students have learned in the section.

 Cycles

 For Further Reflection

Refer to the graph of the speed of a racecar. Describe the appearance of the graph if the racecar ran out of gas at turn 3.

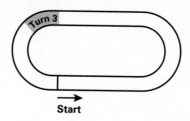

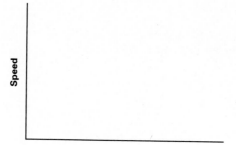

Reaching All Learners

Extension

This would be a good opportunity for students to see that there are mathematical representations for periodic functions, such as sine and cosine. If a graphing calculator with overhead link is available, you may want to show the graphs for sin(x), sin(2x), sin(5x), and so on. Students will explore the right triangle ratios for these trigonometric functions, and tangent, in the unit *Looking at an Angle*.

Solutions and Samples

For Further Reflection

Answers will vary. A graph should show the speed accelerating from the start, slowing at turn 1, increasing out of turn 2 and then slowing down to a stop in turn 3. Students may choose to show one or more laps before the car runs out of gas in turn 3.

Hints and Comments

Overview

Students use the Check Your Work problems as self-assessment. The answers to these problems are provided in the Student Book.

Planning

After finishing Section D, you may assign problems for extra practice from the Additional Practice section on page 51 of the Student Book.

Section Focus

Students already investigated exponential growth in Section C. Each new value was determined by multiplying by a growth factor. In this section, growth factors between zero and one are used to describe exponential decay in real life situations like decrease of the value of a car over time and the absorption of some kind of medicine in the blood stream. The relationship between percents and fractions is applied.

Pacing and Planning

Day 15: Fifty Percent Off		Student pages 43–44
INTRODUCTION	Problems 1–4	Graph and interpret the decrease over time of the value of a car.
CLASSWORK	Problems 5–7	Investigate the decrease in the amount of medicine that remains in a person's stomach at specific intervals of time after ingestion.
HOMEWORK	Problem 8	Make a graph of the medicine absorption data.

Day 16: Comparisons		Student pages 44–46
INTRODUCTION	Review homework.	Review homework from Day 15.
CLASSWORK	Problems 9–12	Investigate other patterns of exponential decay.
HOMEWORK	Check Your Work	Student self-assessment: Describe various situations involving exponential decay.

Day 17: Unit Summary		
INTRODUCTION	Review homework.	Review homework from Day 16.
REVIEW	Sections A–E review	Review Check Your Work and Summary pages from Sections A–E.

Additional Resources: *Algebra Tools*; Additional Practice, Section E, page 51

Materials

Student Resources

No resources required.

Teachers Resources

No resources required.

Student Materials

Quantities listed per student.

- Calculator
- Graph paper (two sheets)

* See Hints and Comments for optional materials.

Learning Lines

Relationships Showing Exponential Growth

Exponential decay is sometimes referred to as *negative growth*. The growth factor is not negative but a decimal or fraction between 0 and 1.

Number Sense

While working through this section, students show their understanding of the relationship between fractions, decimals, and percents. For example, to calculate one-half of the medicine left in the blood stream after ten minutes, students may either multiply the amount by $\frac{1}{2}$, find 50% of the amount, or divide the amount by two since these expressions are equivalent to each other.

At the End of the Section: Learning Outcomes

Students use decimal and fraction growth factors to represent exponential decreasing patterns. They interpret and use tables, graphs, and NEXT-CURRENT formulas to describe exponential decay.

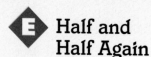

Half and Half Again

Notes

1 You might begin with a class discussion of the context of this problem. Ask students to explain what it means that the car price lowers by 50%.

3 Encourage students to refer to the pattern of decrease in their arguments. They may give examples in dollar amounts. Students should be able to see that the greatest decrease in price occurs during the first two years of a car's life. After that time, the amount of depreciation is less.

Half and Half Again

Fifty Percent Off

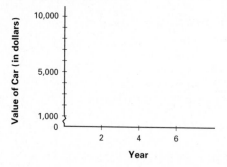

Monica is shopping for a used car. She compares the prices and ages of midsize cars. She notices that adding two years to the age of a car lowers the price by 50%.

1. Copy the diagram below. Graph the value of a $10,000 car over a six-year period.

2. Is the graph linear? Why or why not?

Monica decides she does not want to keep a car for more than two years. She needs advice on whether to buy a new or used car.

3. Write a few sentences explaining what you would recommend. Support your recommendation.

4. a. **Reflect** Show that at this rate, the car never has a zero value.

   b. Is this realistic?

Reaching All Learners

Writing Opportunity

You might have students write a few paragraphs in their journals that explain the pros and cons of buying a new car and of buying a used car. Encourage them to use mathematical reasons.

Solutions and Samples

1.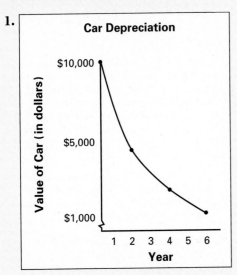

2. No, the graph is not linear. Sample explanation:

The graph is not a straight line because the car's value does not decrease by the same amount every year. Instead, it decreases by a smaller amount each year.

3. Answers will vary. Sample responses:

- Buy a two-year-old used car. The car is almost new, so it will probably look good and run well. Also the car has lost its biggest drop in value, so it won't go down in value as much in the years ahead.

- Buy a new car because all of the parts are new and will last longer. A new car will also have a warranty so that if something goes wrong, you can get it replaced. The big drop in value for a new car might be offset by having the warranty.

4. a. Strategies will vary. Some students may say that extending the graph shows that the curve never reaches the horizontal axis. Other students may say that repeated halving never results in a product of zero, and may use an arrow string to show that even fractional values will never reach zero.

$$1 \xrightarrow{\div 2} \frac{1}{2} \xrightarrow{\div 2} \frac{1}{4} \xrightarrow{\div 2} \frac{1}{8} \xrightarrow{\div 2} \frac{1}{16}$$
$$\xrightarrow{\div 2} \frac{1}{32} \xrightarrow{\div 2} \frac{1}{64} \xrightarrow{\div 2} \frac{1}{128} \xrightarrow{\div 2} \frac{1}{256}$$

b. Answers will vary. Sample responses:

- No, it is not realistic. Some cars may become involved in an accident and be so damaged that you cannot drive them, so these cars have a zero value. Note that some students may argue that the cars can be sold for scrap and so are worth something.

Hints and Comments

Materials

graph paper (one sheet per student)

Overview

Students draw a graph showing the decrease in the value of a car over a six-year period. They also decide whether this process is linear or not.

About the Mathematics

In Section C, students investigated situations that involved exponential growth. Each new value was determined by doubling the original value. In this section, students explore patterns of decrease, known as *exponential decay,* in which the new value is determined by repeatedly halving the original value. The relationship between percents and fractions is stressed in units from the algebra and number strands.

Planning

Students may work in pairs or small groups on problems 1 and 2. Be sure to discuss students' solutions and explanations.

Comments About the Solutions

1. Be sure students understand the basic concept of a repeated percent decrease, or exponential decay. They should be able to use the following relationship between percents and fractions: lowering a price by 50% is the same as taking half of the price.

Yes, it is realistic. Some cars may become collector's items and never reach a value of zero. In fact, their value may increase instead of decrease.

Medicine

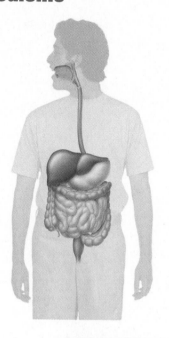

When you take a certain kind of medicine, it first goes to your stomach and then is gradually absorbed into your bloodstream. Suppose that in the first 10 minutes after it reaches your stomach, half of the medicine is absorbed into your bloodstream. In the second 10 minutes, half of the remaining medicine is absorbed, and so on.

6 Encourage students to extend the diagrams they drew for problem 5 to help them answer this question. Suggest that they also include a short explanation that describes how they found their answer.

5. What part of the medicine is still in your stomach after 30 minutes? After 40 minutes? You may use drawings to explain your answer.

6. What part of the medicine is left in your stomach after one hour?

Kendria took a total of 650 milligrams (mg) of this medicine.

7 Students may prefer to do repeated division by two. Have students round the amounts to whole numbers or to the nearest tenth.

7. Copy the table. Fill in the amount of medicine that is still in Kendria's stomach after each ten-minute interval during one hour.

Minutes after Taking Medicine	0	10	20	30	40	50	60
Medicine in Kendria's Stomach (in mg)	650						

8 A complete graph should have a title, and each axis should have a label and a consistent scale. Students may also need to be reminded that time is graphed along the horizontal axis.

8. Graph the information in the table you just completed. Describe the shape of the graph.

The time it takes for something to reduce by half is called its half-life.

9. Is the amount of medicine in Kendria's stomach consistent with your answer to problem 6? Explain.

Assessment Pyramid

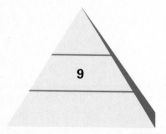

9

Make connections between situation, graph, and table.

Reaching All Learners

Intervention

Check students' graphs for problem 8 while they are working. It is important that students understand that the next amount can be found by taking half of the current amount or by multiplying the current amount by one-half.

Extension

Have students think of other situations where an amount of something decreases over time.

Solutions and Samples

5.

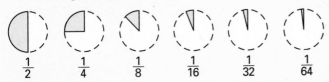

| 0 | 10 | 20 | 30 | 40 minutes |

6. After 60 minutes, there is $\frac{1}{64}$ of the medicine present. Some students might show this with a drawing. Sample drawing:

$\frac{1}{2}$ $\frac{1}{4}$ $\frac{1}{8}$ $\frac{1}{16}$ $\frac{1}{32}$ $\frac{1}{64}$

7.

Minutes after Taking Medicine	0	10	20	30	40	50	60
Medicine in Kendria's Stomach (in mg)	650	325	162.5	81.25	40.625	20.313	10.156

8. See the graph below. Descriptions will vary. Sample descriptions:

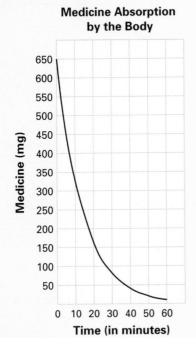

Medicine Absorption by the Body

The graph is falling slower and slower. That is because the amount the body absorbs decreases less and less as time goes by.

9. Students should say yes, because $\frac{1}{64}$ of 650 milligrams is about 10 milligrams.

Hints and Comments

Overview

Students continue to investigate exponential decay within the context of decrease of car value. They investigate the way medicine is absorbed by the bloodstream over time. They make a table of the amount of medicine that remains in a person's stomach after specific time intervals.

About the Mathematics

It is critical that students understand and are able to use the relationships between fractions, decimals, and percents to investigate exponential decay in this section. These connections are also studied in units *Fraction Times* and *More or Less*. For example, to calculate one-half of the medicine amount left after 10 minutes, students may either multiply the amount by $\frac{1}{2}$, find 50% of the amount, or divide the amount by 2, since these expressions are equivalent to one another.

Many students may be able to recognize the similarities between exponential growth, studied in a previous section, and exponential decay. Both situations involve repeated multiplication using a growth or decay factor. In exponential growth, the factor is a number greater than one, while in exponential decay, the factor is a number between zero and one. Students may recall the factors of enlargement or reduction from the unit *Ratios and Rates,* and remember that a factor between zero and one indicates a reduction.

Planning

Discuss students' solutions and strategies, especially for problem 7. Students may work on problems 8 and 9 in pairs or in small groups.

Comments About the Solutions

7. Some students may find the answer by using the fractions from problem 5. For example, after 30 minutes, you have $\frac{1}{8}$ left, and $\frac{1}{8}$ of 650 is 81.25.

8. You might want to discuss with students that the amount decreases by a factor of one-half, or 0.5.

Did You Know?

Some students may ask whether medicine stays in the body for the rest of a person's life. The answer is, of course not. The halving concept used here is an approximate model that is applicable for a limited time period. Most of the medicine will be absorbed in the bloodstream; some of it may never be absorbed and will later be expelled from the body.

Notes

Suppose that Carlos takes 840 mg of another type of medicine. For this medicine, half the amount in his stomach is absorbed into his bloodstream every two hours.

10. Copy and fill in the table to show the amounts of medicine in Carlos's stomach.

Hours after Taking Medicine	0	2	4	6	8	10	12
Medicine in Carlos's Stomach (in mg)	840						

11c Refer students to the table if they are not able to answer this question.

11. a. How are the succeeding entries in the table related to one another?

b. Find a NEXT-CURRENT formula for the amount of medicine in Carlos's stomach.

c. Does the graph show linear growth? Quadratic growth? Explain.

The table in problem 10 shows **negative growth**.

12. a. Reflect Explain what negative growth means.

12a Although *negative growth* sounds like an oxymoron, mathematically it refers to the relationship between negative exponents and values between 0 and 1.

b. What is the growth factor?

c. Do you think the growth factor can be a negative number? Why or why not?

In Section C, you studied examples of exponential growth with whole number growth factors. The example above shows exponential growth with a positive growth factor less than one. This is called **exponential decay**.

Assessment Pyramid

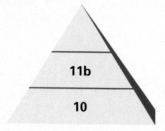

11b

10

Describe exponential decay using recursive formulas.

Understand and use growth factors.

Reaching All Learners

Extension

Some teachers may want to discuss negative exponents in the discussion of negative growth factors. Negative exponents are related to fractions in the following way: $x^{-1} = \frac{1}{x}$ (for example, $2^{-1} = \frac{1}{2}$).

Solutions and Samples

10.

Hours after Taking Medicine	0	2	4	6	8	10	12
Medicine in Carlos's Stomach (in mg)	840	420	210	105	52.5	26.25	13.125

11. a. Each succeeding entry in the column of the table for the medicine in Carlos' stomach is multiplied by $\frac{1}{2}$. The number of hours increases by two each time.

b. NEXT = CURRENT $\times \frac{1}{2}$

c. The graph does not show linear growth because it does not have constant growth. It has the same shape as the graph of problem 8. It is not quadratic as you can see from the first and second differences:

first differences: 420; 210; 105; 52.5; ......

second differences: 210; 105; 52.5; ......

The second differences are not equal.

12. a. Negative growth means that each number is smaller than the previous one.

b. The growth factor is $\frac{1}{2}$.

c. The growth factor cannot be negative. If the amount of medicine in your blood is for instance 840 milligrams, it would be impossible to have a negative number of milligrams of medicine in your stomach later.

Hints and Comments

Materials

graph paper (one sheet per student)

Overview

Students complete a table to make a graph. They then investigate a similar problem about the absorption of medicine into a person's bloodstream. Students find a NEXT-CURRENT formula describing exponential decay within the context of absorption of medicine in the blood stream.

About the Mathematics

In situations involving exponential increase, the *growth factor* is always a number greater than one, while in situations involving exponential decrease, the factor is a number between zero and one. Even though exponential decay is sometimes named *negative growth,* the factor can never be negative.

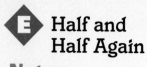

E Half and Half Again

Notes

E Half-Lives

Summary ⟫

You have explored several situations in which amounts have decreased by a factor of $\frac{1}{2}$. For example, the price of a car decreased by a factor of $\frac{1}{2}$ every two years. The amount of medicine in the stomach decreased by a factor of $\frac{1}{2}$ every 10 minutes, or every two hours.

Sometimes things get smaller by half and half again and half again and so on. When things change this way, the change is called *exponential decay*. When amounts decrease by a certain factor, the growth is not linear and not quadratic. You can check by finding the *first* and *second differences*.

Check Your Work ⟫

Suppose you have two substances, A and B. The amount of each substance changes in the following ways over the same length of time:

Substance A: NEXT = CURRENT $\times \frac{1}{2}$

Substance B: NEXT = CURRENT $\times \frac{1}{3}$

1. Are the amounts increasing or decreasing over time?

2. Which of the amounts is changing more rapidly, A or B? Support your answer with a table or a graph.

Although one of the amounts is changing more rapidly, both are decreasing in a similar way.

3. **a.** How would you describe the way they are changing—faster and faster, linearly, or slower and slower? Explain.

   b. **Reflect** What is the mathematical name for this type of change?

For Further Reflection

Write a description of exponential decay using pesticides.

For Further Reflection

The reflection question is meant to summarize and extend what students have learned in the section.

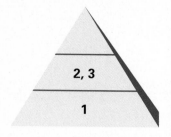

Assessment Pyramid

2, 3

1

Assesses Section E Goals

Reaching All Learners

Extension

Have students make up a problem similar to the two equations on this page, except use $\frac{1}{3}$ and $\frac{1}{4}$ instead of $\frac{1}{2}$ and $\frac{1}{3}$. Have students make a graph and a table for each, and explain what is happening over time.

Parent Involvement

The Summary offers an opportunity for parents to review the unit with their child.

Solutions and Samples

Answers to Check Your Work

1. The amounts are decreasing. Sample explanations:
   - For substance A, after every time interval, half of what there was is left; and for substance B, after every time interval, one-third of what there was is left.
   - You can see the decrease when you use the formulas to make tables.

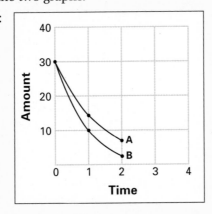

Time	0	1	2
A	30	15	7.5

$\times \frac{1}{2}$ $\times \frac{1}{2}$

Time	0	1	2
B	30	10	3.3

$\times \frac{1}{3}$ $\times \frac{1}{3}$

2. The amount of substance B is decreasing more rapidly. You can see the decrease by looking at the numbers if you make a table for the answer to problem 1. The amount of B goes down faster.

   You can see that substance B is decreasing faster by looking at the two graphs.

   Sample graph:

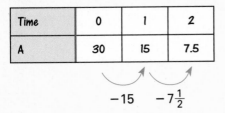

3. a. More and more slowly. Sample explanation:

   You can see that the decrease is happening more and more slowly by looking at the differences in the tables; for example:

Time	0	1	2
A	30	15	7.5

-15 $-7\frac{1}{2}$

Hints and Comments

Overview

Students read and discuss the Summary. They then use the Check Your Work problems as self-assessment. The answers to these problems are provided in the Student Book.

Planning

Read and discuss the Summary with students, focusing on the similarities and differences between exponential increase and decrease. After students finish Section E, you may assign appropriate activities from the Additional Practice section on page 51.

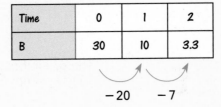

Time	0	1	2
B	30	10	3.3

-20 -7

If you look at the graphs, you can see that the decrease slows down and the graphs become "flatter" over time.

b. This type of change is called exponential decay.

For Further Reflection

Answers will vary. Sample response:

When pesticides are sprayed in a field they are at full strength. Insects on plants are killed right away. But after one week day some new insects come into the area and only half the insects are killed (the pesticide is not at full strength due to the weather). After another week only one fourth of the insects are killed. By the end of the month, the pesticide has lost so much of its strength that the pesticide needs to be reapplied, even though some of the old pesticide is still there!

Additional Practice

Section Ⓐ Trendy Graphs

The graph on the left shows how much the population of the state of Washington grew each decade from 1930 to 2000.

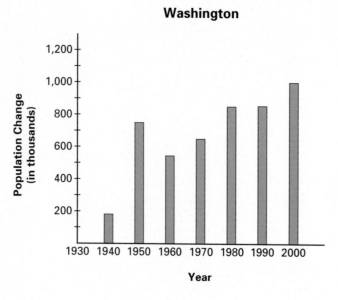

Washington

Population Change (in thousands)

1,200
1,000
800
600
400
200

1930 1940 1950 1960 1970 1980 1990 2000

Year

1. a. By approximately how much did the population grow from 1930 to 1940?

b. In 1930, the population of Washington was 1,563,396. What was the approximate population of Washington in 1940?

2. a. During which decade did the population grow the most? Explain.

b. When did the population grow the least? Explain.

The graph below shows the growth of Alabama's population from 1930 to 2000.

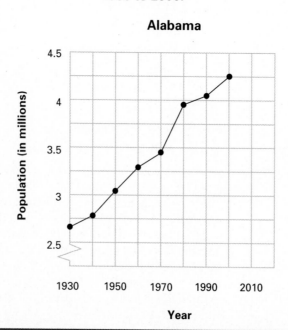

Alabama

Population (in millions)

4.5
4
3.5
3
2.5

1930 1950 1970 1990 2010

Year

3. a. Describe the growth of the population from the year 1960 until the year 2000.

b. From 1970 to 1980, the population of Alabama grew fast. How does the graph show this?

Section A. Trendy Graphs

1. a. The population grew by about 180,000 people. Estimates will vary. Accept estimates in the range of 170,000–190,000 people.

   b. Answers will vary, depending on students' estimates for part **a**. Based on a population growth between 1930 and 1940 of 180,000 people, the population in 1940 was 1,743,396 people (1,563,396 + 180,000 = 1,743,396).

2. a. The population grew the most between 1990 and 2000. Explanations will vary. Sample explanation:

   The graphs show that the greatest change in population, indicated by the longest bar, was during the decade ending in 2000.

   b. The population grew the least between 1930 and 1940. Explanations will vary. Sample explanation:

   The smallest increase in population was during the decade ending in 1940 and is indicated by the shortest bar on the graph.

3. a. Descriptions will vary. Sample description:

   From 1960 to 1970, the growth of the population of Alabama slowed down slightly compared to the previous years.

   From 1970 to 1980, the growth was considerably larger than in the previous decade, but from 1980 to 1990 the population grew only little, about the same change as during the decade of 1930 to 1940.

   b. Explanations will vary. Sample explanation:

   The graph line connecting the two dots representing 1970 and 1980 is very steep.

Additional Practice

These are two pictures of the same iguana.

The chart shows the length of the iguana as it grew.

Date	Length (in inches)	
	Overall	**Body (without tail)**
July 2004	$11\frac{1}{2}$	3
August 2004	13	$3\frac{1}{2}$
September 2004	15	4
October 2004	17	5
November 2004	$21\frac{1}{2}$	$5\frac{1}{2}$
January 2005	27	$7\frac{1}{2}$
March 2005	$29\frac{1}{2}$	$8\frac{1}{2}$
April 2005	31	9
June 2005	$38\frac{1}{2}$	$11\frac{1}{2}$
August 2005	45	14
October 2005	$49\frac{1}{2}$	$15\frac{1}{2}$
December 2005	50	$15\frac{1}{2}$

Note that the iguana was not measured every single month.

Section A. Trendy Graphs
(continued)

There are no problems to solve on this page.

The graph of the length of the iguana's body, without the tail, is drawn below.

Growth of an Iguana

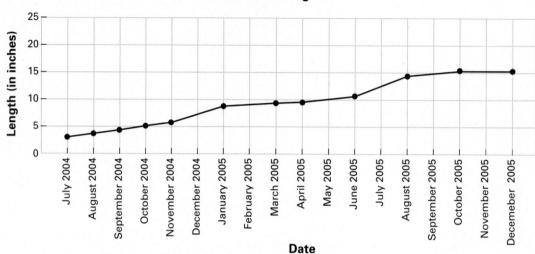

4. **a.** Use graph paper to draw the line graph of the overall length of the iguana. Be as accurate as possible.

   b. Use your graph to estimate the overall birth length of the iguana in June 2004.

   c. On November 1, 2005, the iguana lost part of its tail. Use a different color to show what the graph of the overall length may have looked like between October and December 2005.

Section B Linear Patterns

Mark notices that the height of the water in his swimming pool is low; it is only 80 cm high. He starts to fill up the pool with a hose. One hour later, the water is 95 cm high.

1. If Mark continues to fill his pool at the same rate, how deep will the water be in one more hour?

2. **a.** If you know the current height of the water, how can you find what the height will be in one hour?

   b. Write a NEXT-CURRENT formula for the height of the water.

3. Mark wants to fill his pool to 180 cm. How much time will this take? Explain.

Section A. Trendy Graphs (continued)

4. a. Sample graph:

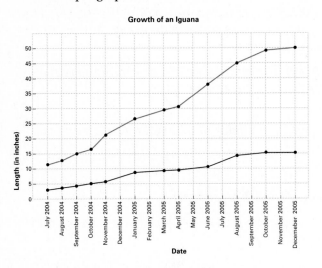

b. Accept answers between 8–10.

c. Sample graph:

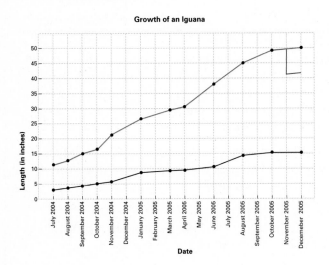

Section B. Linear Patterns

1. 110 cm

2. a. Add 15 cm to the current height of the water.

   b. NEXT = CURRENT + 15

3. It will take 6 hours and 40 minutes to fill the pool to a height of 180 cm. Explanations will vary. Sample explanation:

Mark wants to raise the water level of the pool to 180 cm. The current water level is 80 cm, so he needs to raise the water level 100 cm. The water level rises 15 cm per hour. I divided to find the answer. $100 \div 15 = 6\frac{2}{3}$, which equals six hours and 40 minutes.

Additional Practice

Mark has already spent three hours filling up his pool. He wants to fill up the pool faster, so he uses another hose. With the two hoses, the water level rises 25 cm every hour.

4. On graph paper, draw a graph showing the height of the water in Mark's pool after he starts using two hoses.

The following formula gives the height of the water in Mark's pool after he starts using two hoses.

$$H = \underline{\hspace{1cm}} + 25T$$

5. a. What do the letters H and T represent?

    b. A number is missing in the formula. Rewrite the formula and fill in the missing number.

    c. If Mark had not used a second hose, how would the formula in part **b** be different?

Section ⓒ Differences in Growth

Food in a restaurant must be carefully prepared to prevent the growth of harmful bacteria. Food inspectors analyze the food to check its safety. Suppose that federal standards require restaurant food to contain fewer than 100,000 salmonella bacteria per gram and that, at room temperature, salmonella has a growth factor of two per hour.

1. There are currently 200 salmonella bacteria in 1 g of a salad. In how many hours will the number of bacteria be over the limit if the salad is left at room temperature?

A food inspector found 40,000,000 salmonella bacteria in 1 g of chocolate mousse that had been left out of the refrigerator.

2. Assume that the mousse had been left at room temperature the entire time. What level of bacteria would the food inspector have found for the chocolate mousse one hour earlier? One hour later?

3. Write a NEXT-CURRENT formula for the number of salmonella bacteria in a gram of food kept at room temperature.

4. When the chocolate mousse was removed from the refrigerator, it had a safe level of salmonella bacteria. How many hours before it was inspected could it have been removed from the refrigerator?

Section B. Linear Patterns (continued)

4. See the graph below. Since Mark has been filling the pool for three hours at 15 cm per hour (3 × 15 = 45 cm), the graph for filling the pool with two hoses starts at 80 cm + 45 cm, or 125 cm.

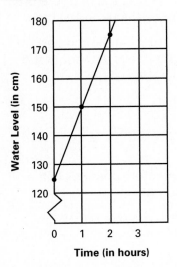

5. a. *H* stands for the height of the water. *T* stands for the amount of time in hours that two hoses have been filling the pool.

   b. $H = 125 + 25T$

   c. $H = 125 + 15T$; T would be multiplied by 15 instead of 25. Some students may write a formula using 80 cm as the starting height of the water. In that case, the answer would be $H = 80 + 15T$

Section C. Differences in Growth

1. The amount of bacteria will be over the limit in a little less than nine hours.

Hours	0	1	2	3	4	5	6	7	8	9
Number of Bacteria	200	400	800	1,600	3,200	6,400	12,800	25,600	51,200	102,400

2. The inspector would have found 20,000,000 bacteria one hour earlier.

   The inspector would have found 80,000,000 bacteria one hour later.

3. NEXT = CURRENT × 2

4. The chocolate mousse was removed from the refrigerator almost 9 hours before it was inspected. Strategies will vary. Some students may count how many times they must divide by 2 until the quantity of bacteria is under 100,000.

Section **D** Cycles

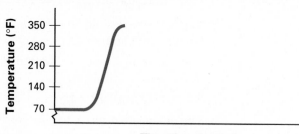

Temperature (°F)

350
280
210
140
70

Time (in minutes)

The graph shows the temperature of an oven over a period of time.

1. Describe what the red part of the graph tells you about the temperature of the oven.

2. Copy the graph and show how the temperature changes in the oven as the heating element shuts on and off.

3. Show what happens when someone turns the oven off.

4. Color one cycle on your graph.

Section **E** Half and Half Again

Boiling water (water at 100°C) cools down at a rate determined by the air temperature. Suppose the temperature of the water decreases by a factor of $\frac{1}{10}$ every minute if the air temperature is 0°C.

1. Under the above conditions, what is the temperature of boiling water one minute after it has started to cool down? Two minutes after? Three? Four?

Examine the following NEXT-CURRENT formulas.

2. Which ones give the temperature for water that is cooling down if the air temperature is 0°C? Explain.

   a. NEXT = CURRENT − 10

   b. NEXT = CURRENT × 0.9

   c. NEXT = CURRENT − CURRENT × 0.1

   d. NEXT = CURRENT × 0.1

3. How long does it take for boiling water to cool down to 40°C if the air temperature is 0°C?

Section D. Cycles

1. Answers will vary. Sample response:

   Before the oven is turned on, the oven temperature stays at room temperature. After the oven is turned on, the temperature rises rapidly until it reaches 350 degrees.

2.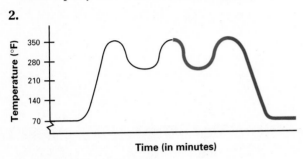

3. See the green portion of the graph in the solution to problem 2.

4. See the red portion of the graph in the solution to problem 2.

Section E. Half and Half Again

1. The temperature of boiling water after cooling down for 1 minute is 90°C; after 2 minutes 81°C; after 3 minutes 72.9°C (or about 73°C); after 4 minutes 65.61°C (or about 66°C).

2. **a.** This formula is not correct. Explanations will vary. Sample explanation:

   The formula does not hold true when the CURRENT is 90; $90 - 10 = 80$ and not 81. Subtracting 10 is not the same as decreasing by $\frac{1}{10}$.

   b. This formula is correct. Sample explanation:

   $0.9 \times 100 = 90$

   $0.9 \times 90 = 81$

   $0.9 \times 81 = 72.9$

   c. This formula is correct. Sample explanation:

   $100 - 0.1 \times 100 = 100 - 10 = 90$

   $90 - 0.1 \times 90 = 90 - 9 = 81$

   d. This formula is not correct. Sample explanation:

   $0.1 \times 100 = 10$ and not 90. You need to subtract the 10 from the 100.

3. It takes boiling water somewhere between 8 and 9 minutes to cool down to a temperature of 40°C. Sample explanation:

   I used the formula NEXT = CURRENT × 0.9 and made a table to show my answers.

Minute	0	1	2	3	4	5	6	7	8	9
Temperature (°C)	100	90	81	72.9	65.6	59	53.1	47.8	43	38.7

Assessment Overview

Unit assessments in *Mathematics in Context* include two quizzes and a Unit Test. Quiz 1 is to be used anytime after students have completed Section B. Quiz 2 can be used after students have completed Section D. The Unit Test addresses all of the major goals of the unit. You can evaluate student responses to these assessments to determine what each student knows about the content goals addressed in this unit.

Pacing

Each quiz is designed to take approximately 25 minutes to complete. The Unit Test is designed to be completed during a 45-minute class period. For more information on how to use these assessments, see the Planning Assessment section on the next page.

Goal	Assessment Opportunities		Problem Levels
• Use information about increase and/or decrease to create line graphs.	Quiz 1 Test	Problems 1ad Problems 1a, 5c	
• Identify and describe patterns of increase and/or decrease from a table or graph.	Quiz 1 Quiz 2 Test	Problems 1abc Problem 2b Problems 2abcd, 3abc, 5b	
• Identify characteristics of periodic graphs.	Quiz 2 Test	Problem 2a Problems 4abc	Level I
• Identify linear patterns in tables and graphs.	Quiz 1 Test	Problem 1c Problems 3abc, 5bc	
• Understand and use growth factors.	Quiz 2 Test	Problems 1ac Problem 5a	
• Describe linear, quadratic, and exponential growth with recursive formulas.	Quiz 2 Test	Problem 1d Problem 5e	
• Describe linear growth with direct formulas.	Quiz 1 Test	Problems 2ab Problem 1b	
• Make connections between situation, graph, and table.	Quiz 1 Quiz 2 Test	Problems 2cd Problem 2b Problems 2d, 3d, 4de, 5bcd	Level II
• Reason about situations of growth in terms of slope, maximum and minimum range, decrease, and increase.	Test	Problems 2d, 5a	
• Recognize the power of graphs and/or tables for representing and solving problems.	Test	Problem 5d	
• Use algebraic models to represent realistic situations.	Quiz 2 Test	Problem 1b Problem 5e	Level III

About the Mathematics

These assessment activities assess the major goals of the *Ups and Downs* unit. Refer to the Goals and Assessment Opportunities section on the previous page for information regarding the goals that are assessed in each problem. Some of the problems that involve multiple skills and processes address more than one unit goal. To assess students' ability to engage in non-routine problem solving (a Level III goal in the Assessment Pyramid), some problems assess students' ability to use their skills and conceptual knowledge in new situations. For example, in the radioactivity problem on the Unit Test (problem 5), students must integrate their understanding of exponential decay and use of graphs and recursive formulas to solve a new problem.

Planning Assessment

These assessments are designed for individual assessment; however, some problems can be done in pairs or small groups. It is important that students work individually if you want to evaluate each student's understanding and abilities.

Make sure you allow enough time for students to complete the problems. If students need more than one class sessions to complete the problems, it is suggested that they finish during the next mathematics class, or you may assign select problems as a take-home activity. Students should be free to solve the problems their own way. Student use of calculators is at the teacher's discretion.

If individual students have difficulties with any particular problems, you may give the student the option of making a second attempt after providing him or her a hint. You may also decide to use one of the optional problems or Extension activities not previously done in class as additional assessments for students who need additional help.

Scoring

Solution and scoring guides are included for each quiz and the Unit Test. The method of scoring depends on the types of questions on each assessment. A holistic scoring approach could also be used to evaluate an entire quiz.

Several problems require students to explain their reasoning or justify their answers. For these questions, the reasoning used by students in solving the problems as well as the correctness of the answers should be considered in your scoring and grading scheme.

Student progress toward goals of the unit should be considered when reviewing student work. Descriptive statements and specific feedback are often more informative to students than a total score or grade. You might choose to record descriptive statements of select aspects of student work as evidence of student progress toward specific goals of the unit that you have identified as essential.

Use additional paper as needed.

1. In newspapers, you often find headlines like these.

> **Population of Seattle Growing Faster and Faster**

> **Price of Calculators Dropping Faster and Faster**

Four different graphs are shown.

A 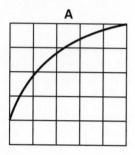 **B** 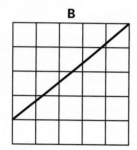 **C** 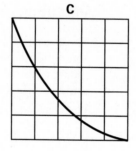 **D**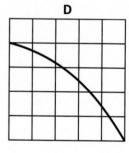

a. Does one of the graphs fit the headline on the left?
If yes, which one?

b. Does one of the graphs fit the headline on the right?
If yes, which one?

c. Make up headlines for the other graphs.

2. Julie wants to get her fence painted. She can choose between two painting businesses, "The ColorFull Company" and "DeLux Painters."

ColorFull has this advertisement: **We charge $20 for the paint and $10 per hour!**

DeLux advertises with this: **Only $15 per hour. Paint included!**

a. Write a direct formula for the price for ColorFull.

b. Write a direct formula for the price for DeLux.

c. The painter for this job will work about three hours. Which painting business should Julie choose and why?

d. DeLux changes their formula to *Price* = 10 + 20 × *hours.* Should Julie change her choice? Why, or why not?

Ups and Downs Quiz 2

Use additional paper as needed.

1. The growth of a certain leaf is described in the table below.

Number of Weeks	1	2	3	4
Area (in cm^2)	2	4	8	

a. Assume the growth in the table above is quadratic, and find the missing value. Show or explain how you found the missing value.

b. Check if the following formula describes the quadratic growth for the leaf described in the table above. Correct the formula if necessary.

$$y = x^2 - x$$

c. Fill in the missing value below for another leaf that grows exponentially.

Number of Weeks	1	2	3	4
Area (in cm^2)	2	4	8	

d. Write a NEXT-CURRENT formula to describe the exponential growth.

Mathematics in Context

2. Ships without radar or other modern equipment on board can find their way at night by using light signals from lighthouses. Every lighthouse has its own light signal, so a captain can identify a lighthouse from the pattern of the light flashes.

Below, you see a graphical representation of one lighthouse's signal pattern.

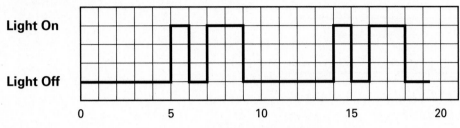

Time (in seconds)

a. Examine the diagram of the lighthouse signal pattern. Shade the diagram to show one cycle of the signal pattern. How long is one period?

b. How many light flashes would you see in a one-minute period?

Use additional paper as needed.

1. In the small town of Bakersfield, there are two taxicab companies. The Metro Taxi Company charges customers a flat rate of $4 per mile. The Acme Taxi Company uses the following table to show their cab fare costs.

Distance (in miles)	1	2	3	4
Cost (in dollars)	7	9	11	13

a. Draw a graph for *each* taxi company showing the costs of cab rides for various distances.

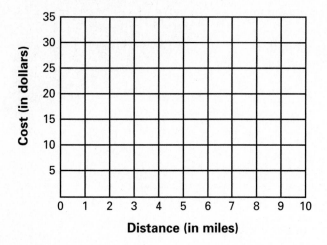

b. Write formulas that could be used to calculate the costs of cab rides using the two taxi companies. Use the letter *C* to represent the cost of the trip and the letter *D* to represent the distance in miles.

2. On the right, you see patterns that are made using matches. The first figure, with one row, is made using 3 matches. The second one, with two rows, is made using 9 matches.

   a. How many matches are used for the third figure, with three rows?

   b. Draw the fourth and fifth figures.

   c. Complete the following table.

Figure 1

Row 1

Figure 2

Row 1
Row 2

Figure 3

Row 1
Row 2
Row 3

Figure Number	1	2	3	4	5	6
Number of Total Matches	3	9				

   d. Is the relationship between the number of rows and the number of matches linear, quadratic, or exponential? Explain your answer.

Use additional paper as needed.

3. On the right is another pattern made using matches.
The first figure, with one row, is made using 2 matches.
Figure 2, with two rows, is made using 6 matches.

a. How many matches are used for the
third, the fourth, and the fifth figure?

third figure: _____

fourth figure: _____

fifth figure: _____

b. Complete the following table.

Figure Number	1	2	3	4	5	6
Number of Total Matches	2	6				

c. Is the relationship between the number of rows and the
number of matches linear, quadratic or exponential? Explain
your answer.

Figure 1

Row 1

Figure 2

Row 1
Row 2

Figure 3

Row 1
Row 2
Row 3

Figure 4

Row 1
Row 2
Row 3
Row 4

Figure 5

Row 1
Row 2
Row 3
Row 4
Row 5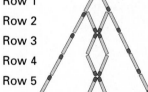

4. The graph shows how the water depth in a coastal harbor changes over time.

Harbor Tides for July 9

(graph showing water depth in meters versus time, with periodic wave peaking at 6 m around 6 A.M. and 6 P.M., dipping to 4 m around 12 P.M.)

Water Depth (in m)

6 A.M.　　12 P.M.　　6 P.M.　　12 A.M.

Time

a. Why is this a periodic graph?

b. Color one cycle of the graph.

c. How long is one period of the graph?

d. The captain of an oil tanker wants to know at what time the next day (July 10) the water will be at its maximum depth. How can he find this out?

e. When will the maximum water depth occur on July 10?

Use additional paper as needed.

5. Nuclear waste is highly radioactive, and it is therefore unsafe for living things. Nuclear waste must be kept in a safe place away from people, animals, and food and water supplies until it loses its dangerous level of radioactivity. Suppose that a nuclear plant produced radioactive waste that would lose its radioactivity as follows: every ten years, the amount of radio-activity decreases by 25%.

One scientist suggested that the nuclear waste be safely stored in barrels for a period of 40 years until it is no longer radioactive. Then the barrels could be dumped into the ocean without causing any harm to humans, marine life, or food and water supplies.

a. How might the scientist have determined that it would take 40 years for the nuclear waste to lose its radioactivity? Do you agree with his plan? Explain your reasoning.

b. The nuclear waste material showed a radioactivity level of 1,024 counts per minute on a Geiger counter. Complete the table below to show how the amount of radioactivity would change over time.

Years	0	10	20		
Counts per Minute	1,024				

c. Make a graph showing the amount of radioactivity over time.

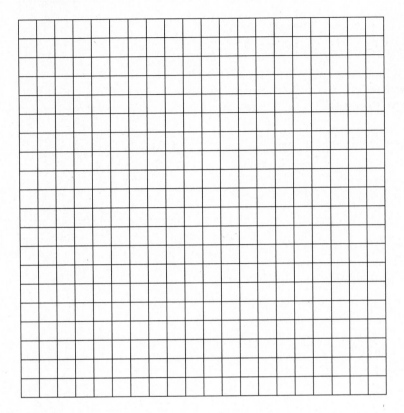

d. Give an estimate of the amount of radioactivity that still remains after 40 years.

e. Write a NEXT-CURRENT formula to describe the decreasing amount of radioactivity in this situation.

Ups and Downs Quiz 1
Solution and Scoring Guide

Possible student answer	Suggested number of score points	Problem level
1. a. No graph fits the headline "faster and faster."	1	I
b. Graph D: "dropping faster and faster" The vertical differences are larger as you move to the right.	1	I
c. Answers will vary. Sample responses: Graph A: "The jump in gas prices is slowing down" Graph B: "Prices of groceries have increased the same amount every year" Graph C: "Decline in fresh water levels is slowing down"	3	I
2. a. *price = 20 + 10 × (number of hours)*	2	II
b. *price = 15 × (number of hours)*	2	II
c. 3 hours: ColorFull will cost 20 + 10 × 3 = $50; DeLux will cost 15 × 3 = $45. She should choose DeLux because this one is the cheapest.	3	II
d. She should probably switch to ColorFull since DeLux will now cost 10 + 20 × 3 = $70, which is more expensive.	3	II
Total score points	15	

Possible student answer	Suggested number of score points	Problem level
1. a. 	2	I

Number of Weeks	1	2	3	4
Area (in cm²)	2	4	8	14

+2 +4 +6

+2 +2

Possible student answer	Suggested number of score points	Problem level
b. $y = x^2 - x$ is not correct. If you evaluate the equation for 1 week, when x *(number of weeks)* is 1, y *(area)* is 0. However, the table shows that when the number of weeks (x) is 1, the area (y) is 2. The correct direct formula is $y = x^2 - x + 2$. This formula can be verified by substituting other values for x.	2	II
c.	2	I

Number of Weeks	1	2	3	4
Area (in cm²)	2	4	8	16

×2 ×2 ×2

Possible student answer	Suggested number of score points	Problem level
d. NEXT = CURRENT × 2	1	II
2. a.	2	I

Light On

Light Off

0   5   10   15   20

Time (in seconds)

Possible student answer	Suggested number of score points	Problem level
One period is nine seconds.	2	I
b. You would see 13 flashes during a one-minute period. Sample explanation: during the first 54 seconds, you would see 6 complete cycles of two flashes, or 12 flashes. During the next 6 seconds, you would see one flash of the next cycle, so altogether, 13 flashes.	3	I/II
Total score points	14	

Ups and Downs Unit Test
Solution and Scoring Guide

Solutions	Score Points	Level
1. a.	2	I
b. Metro: $C = 4D$ Acme: $C = 5 + 2D$	2	II
2. a. 18 matches	1	I
b. Figure 4 Figure 5	2	I
c.	2	I
d. The relationship is quadratic because the second differences are all equal.	3 **1** (answer) **2** (explanation)	I/II

1. a.

Cost (in dollars) vs Distance (in miles)

Metro Taxi Co.
Acme Taxi Co.

2. c.

Figure Number	1	2	3	4	5	6
Number of Total Matches	3	9	18	30	45	63

d.

Figure Number	1	2	3	4	5	6
Number of Total Matches	3	9	18	30	45	63

+ 6 + 9 + 12 + 15 + 18

+ 3 + 3 + 3 + 3

Solutions	Score Points	Level
3. a. 10, 14, and 18 matches	3	I
b.	2	I

Figure Number	1	2	3	4	5	6
Number of Total Matches	2	6	10	14	18	22

Solutions	Score Points	Level
c. linear; the first differences are all the same: +4.	2	I/II
4. a. This is a periodic graph because it shows a repeating pattern.	1	I
b. Answers will vary. Sample response:	2	I

Harbor Tides for July 9

Solutions	Score Points	Level
c. One period is about 14 hours.	1	I
d. Strategies will vary. Sample strategies: The captain can extend the graph and draw the repeating pattern for the next day. The captain can add 14 hours to the last maximum depth time on July 9th. (6:00 P.M. + 14 hours = 8:00 A.M.)	2	II
e. The water will be at its maximum depth at 8:00 A.M. and at 10:00 P.M.	1	II

Solutions	Score Points	Level
5. a. The students should be able to explain the scientists reasoning (1 pt); however, they should also recognize that this type of reasoning is incorrect (1 pt).	2	I/II*

5. a. The students should be able to explain the scientists reasoning (1 pt); however, they should also recognize that this type of reasoning is incorrect (1 pt).

Explanations will vary:
Some students may say that it is incorrect for the scientist to reason that if 25% of the radiation disappears every 10 years, then all of the radiation will be gone in 40 years (4 × 10 = 40).

Some students may show a correct interpretation of decay in radioactive counts to justify their disagreement with the scientist's plan. Example:
Suppose that the starting amount was 100 counts per minute. In 10 years, you will have 75 counts per minute. In 20 years, you will have 56 counts per minute, and in 40 years, you will have 32 counts per minute.

b. Tables will vary depending on students' interpretation of the scientist's reasoning. Give full credit for a table that is completed correctly, in line with the student agreement or disagreement with the scientists' reasoning from part **a**.
Sample response (disagrees with scientist):

Years	0	10	20	30	40
Counts per Minute	1,024	768	576	432	324

Sample response (agrees with scientist):

Years	0	10	20	30	40
Counts per Minute	1,024	512	256	128	0

(Score Points for part b: 2 — Level I/II)*

Ups and Downs Unit Test
Solution and Scoring Guide

Solutions	Score Points	Level
c. Students should receive full credit for a graph that matches the table they completed for part **b**.	2	I/II*

Radioactive Decay

d. Estimates will vary, depending on the graph created. Give student credit for correct interpretation of graph from part **c**. Sample estimates: About 30% of the radioactivity remains. or A Geiger counter would register about 324 counts per minute of radioactivity.	2	II/III*
e. NEXT-CURRENT formulas may vary. Sample formulas: NEXT = 0.75 × CURRENT NEXT = $\frac{3}{4}$ × CURRENT NEXT = CURRENT − (0.25 × CURRENT) NEXT = CURRENT − ($\frac{1}{4}$ × CURRENT) Note: The last two formulas will be correct whether or not students use parentheses.	2	II/III*
		* Differences in the level of reasoning for 5a−5d are due to whether students interpret the situation as linear or exponential.
Total score points	36	

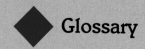

Glossary

The Glossary defines all vocabulary words indicated in this unit. It includes the mathematical terms that may be new to students, as well as words having to do with the contexts introduced in the unit. (Note: The Student Book has no Glossary. Instead, students are encouraged to construct their own definitions, based on their personal experiences with the unit activities.)

The definitions below are specific for the use of the terms in this unit. The page numbers given are from the Student Books.

coring (p. 2) a process to extract material to determine its composition, frequently used with plants, soil, and ice. The core sample extracted through this process is often used to investigate changes in local growth patterns, climate, etc.

cycle (p. 38) the portion of a periodic graph that is repeated

direct formula (p. 17) a formula that can be used to find a value for any given

exponential decay (p. 45) the growth factor of an exponential relationship that lies between 0 and 1

exponential growth (p. 31) the growth factor of an exponential relationship that is greater than 1

growth factor (p. 30) the number by which each current value of an exponential relationship is multiplied to find the next value. The growth factor is always a positive number.

line graph (p. 5) represents a continuous process, occurring over time. Only the dots on the graph, representing data, are meaningful. The straight lines that connect the dots are used to show a trend.

linear growth (p. 9) a growth pattern showing equal increase or decrease over equal (time) periods. A graph of linear growth is a straight line. In a table, if equal periods are used, the first differences are equal.

negative growth (p. 45) a pattern of change in which the dimensions measured are decreasing

NEXT-CURRENT formula (p. 16) a type of formula based on additive or multiplicative differences between successive values (also called a *recursive formula*)

parabola (TG, Section C opener) a bowl-shaped graph. The graph of a quadratic relationship is parabolic.

period (p. 38) the amount of time it takes to repeat one cycle of a periodic graph

periodic graph (p. 38) a graph that has a repeating shape or pattern

photosynthesis (p. 23) a process where plants use sunlight (or other light sources) to synthesize chemical compounds

quadratic (p. 27) a relationship in which the first differences of table values are not equal and the second differences are equal.

second differences (p. 25) the difference between first difference values, often used to test if a relationship is quadratic

steepness (p 19T) equal increase or decrease over equal (time) periods as shown in the graph representing a linear relationship. The higher the increase per period, the steeper the graph.

BRITANNICA
**Mathematics
in
Context**

Blackline
Masters

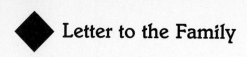
Dear Family,

Your child is about to begin working on the *Mathematics in Context* unit *Ups and Downs*. This algebra unit presents real-world contexts that can be represented by graphs that show change over time.

Students investigate graphs of ocean tides, tree growth, temperature changes, blood pressure, radioactive decay, and so on. They gain an understanding of what the shape of a graph means. Why might a graph go only upward or downward? Students learn to identify cycles (the repeating parts of graphs) and periods (the durations of the parts that repeat).

You can help you child learn about graphs that show change over time by pointing them out when you see them in newspapers or magazines. You may wish to keep track of the temperatures over a week or a month and then create a graph that represents the data you have collected. You can also graph the temperature predictions that your local weather person makes and see how the graphs of the predicted and actual temperatures compare.

We hope you enjoy discussing the uses of graphs and the stories behind them with your child.

Sincerely,

The Mathematics in Context Development Team

Dear Student,

Welcome to *Ups and Downs*. In this unit, you will look at situations that change over time, such as blood pressure or the tides of an ocean. You will learn to represent these changes using tables, graphs, and formulas.

Graphs of temperatures and tides show up-and-down movement, but some graphs, such as graphs for tree growth or melting ice, show only upward or only downward movement.

As you become more familiar with graphs and the changes that they represent, you will begin to notice and understand graphs in newspapers, magazines, and advertisements.

During the next few weeks, look for graphs and statements about growth, such as "Fast-growing waterweeds in lakes become a problem." Bring to class interesting graphs and newspaper articles and discuss them.

Telling a story with a graph can help you understand the story.

Sincerely,

The Mathematics in Context Development Team

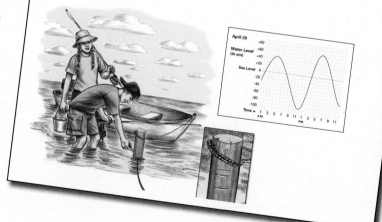

6.

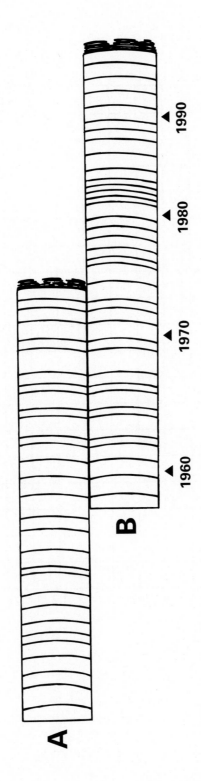
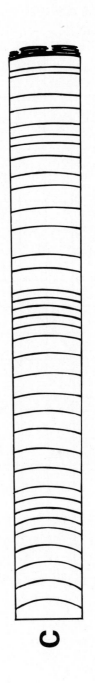

◆ **Student Activity Sheet 2**
Use with *Ups and Downs*, page 5.

Name _____

12. a.

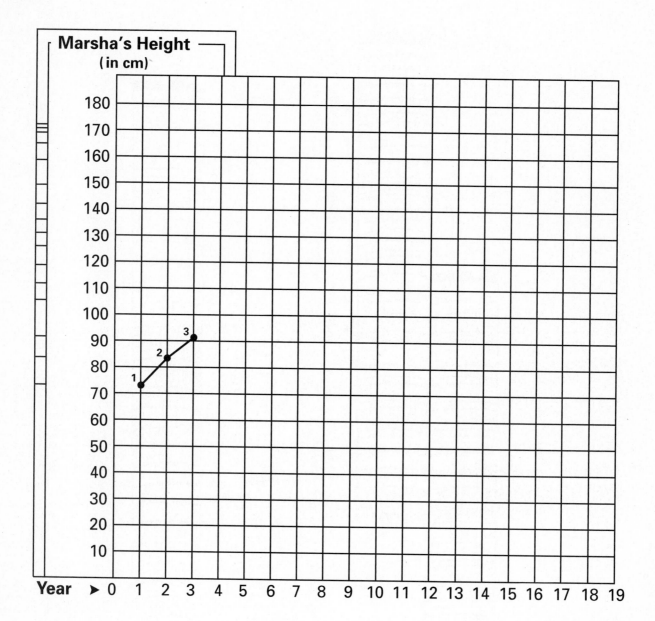

Name_____

Student Activity Sheet 3 ◆
Use with *Ups and Downs*, page 7.

17.

Weight Growth Chart for Boys
Age: Birth to 36 months

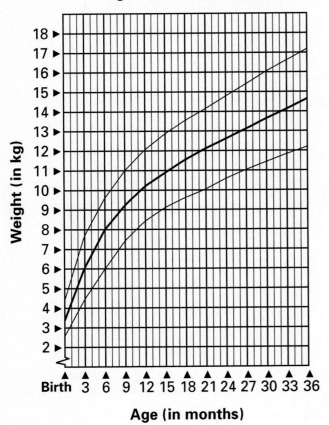

Height Growth Chart for Boys
Age: Birth to 36 months

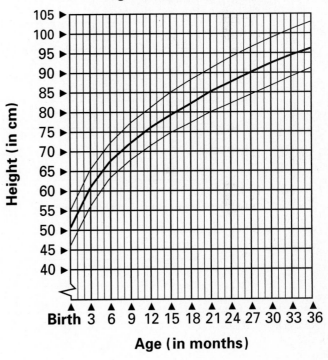

© Am. J. Nutr. American Society for Clinical Nutrition

◆ Student Activity Sheet 4
Use with *Ups and Downs*, page 11.

Name _____

2.

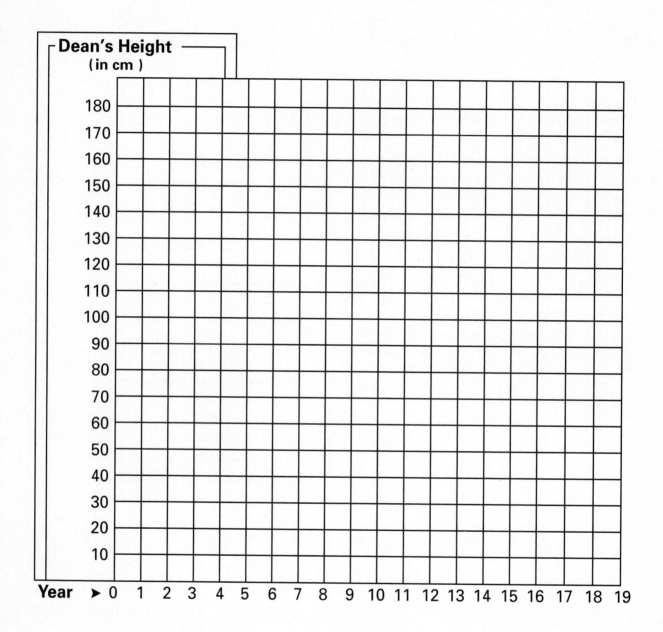

Name _____

Student Activity Sheet 5 ◆
Use with *Ups and Downs*,
pages 14 and 15.

2.b.

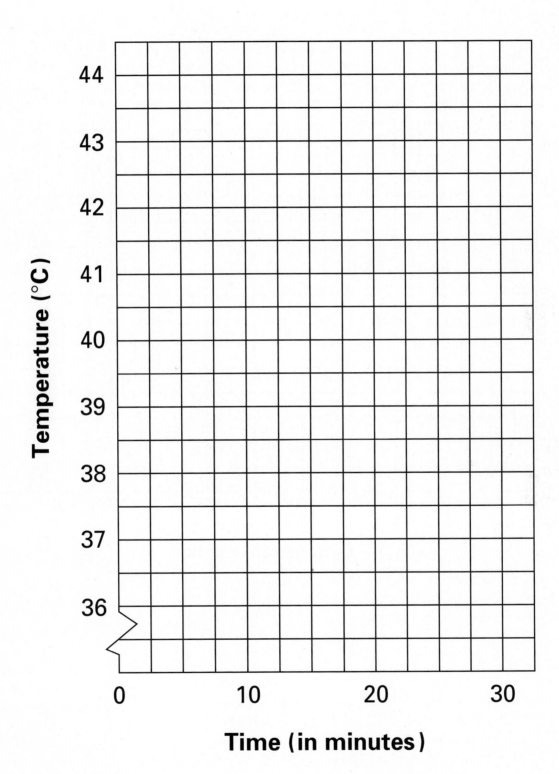

Time (in minutes)

◆ **Student Activity Sheet 6**
Use with *Ups and Downs*, page 19.

Name _____

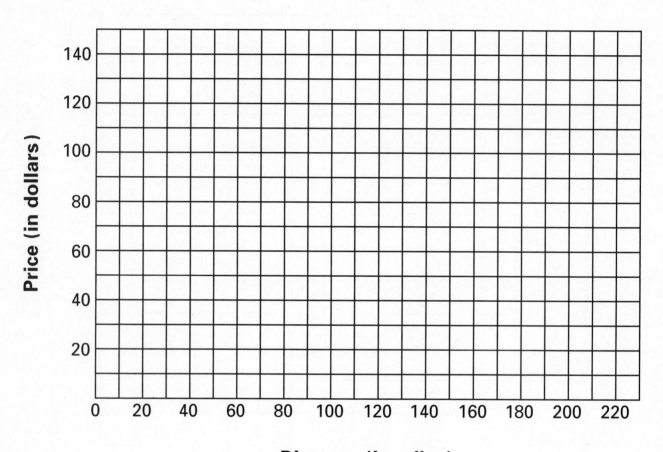

Distance (in miles)

(y-axis: Price (in dollars))

Height (in cm)	6	7	8	9	10	11	12
Area (in cm²)	18	24.5					

Height (in cm)	6	7	8	9	10	11	12
Area (in cm²)	18	24.5	32	-----	-----	-----	-----

First Difference   6.5   7.5   -----   -----   -----   -----

Second Difference   1   -----   -----   -----   -----

◆ Student Activity Sheet 8
Use with *Ups and Downs*, page 25.

Name _____

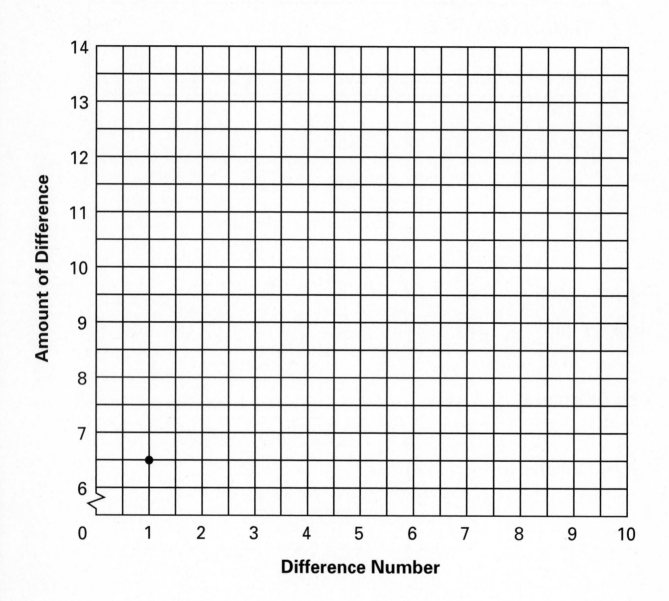

Difference Number

Amount of Difference

9. a. Fill in the remaining area values in the table. Use this formula:
$$A = \tfrac{1}{2}h^2$$

b. Graph the formula on the grid. Why do you think the graph curves upward?

c. Using your graph, estimate the areas of poplar leaves with the following heights: 5.5 cm, 9.3 cm, and 11.7 cm.

Height (in cm)	1	2	3	4	5	6	7	8
Area (in cm²)	0.5	2	4.5					

Area of Black Poplar Leaves

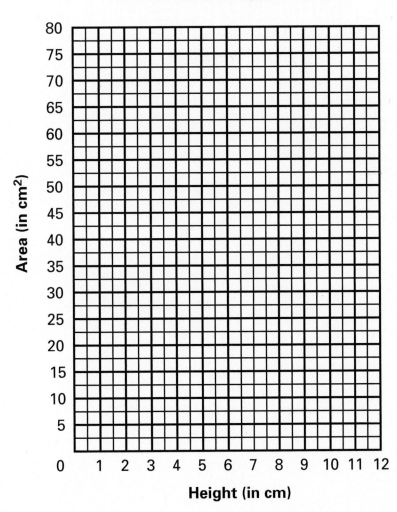

Height (in cm)

Name _____

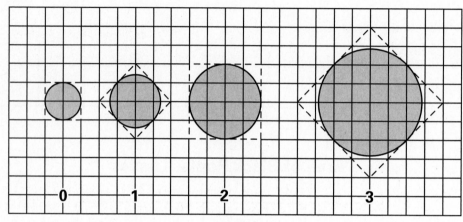

Week

Name _____

Student Activity Sheet 11 ◆
Use with *Ups and Downs*, page 30.

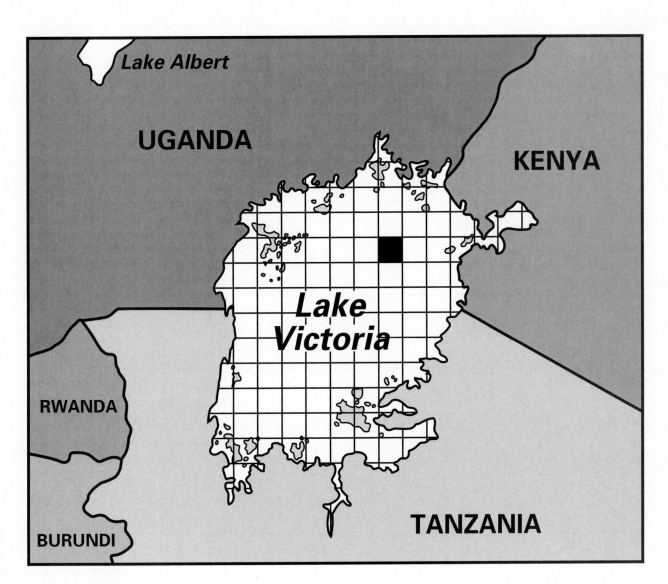

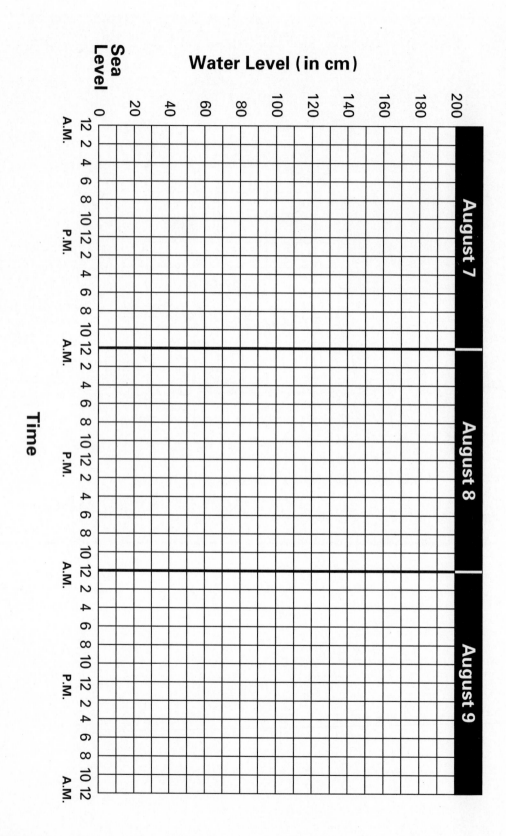

Name _____

Student Activity Sheet 13 ◆
Use with *Ups and Downs*, page 38.

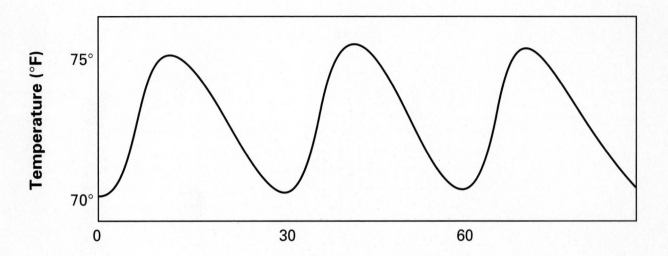

9. b. Color one cycle on the graph.